Cosmic Calligraphy   Born Free

written by
Born Free

Cosmic Calligraphy   Born Free

Carl Born Free Wharton
Cosmic Calligraphy

All rights reserved. Printed in the United States of America.
No part of this book can be reproduced
in any written, electronic, digital, recording,
or photocopying form without the explicit
permission by the author or the publisher.
The only exception is in the case of reprints
in the context of reviews.

front cover created with the online program
Photo Lab
Follow @ https://photolab.me/

ISBN: 9798541952247

Follow on all social media platforms #therealbornfree

Copyright © 2021 Conscious Commentary Publishing LLC /
Independently Published

God gave you a voice, use it!

Previous books by Born Free (Available on Amazon.com)

The Book of Born Free
The Wisdom of Living Right Now!
Volume One

Morning Wake Up Calls

Panther Poetry

The Book of Born Free
The Wisdom of Living Right Now!
Volume Two

A Citizen's Guide to Balancing *unbalanced*
POWER relationships
(Warnings & Instructions)

Schemers

Verses of Wine

Pyroclastic Flow

Cosmic Calligraphy   Born Free

**Other books Published by
Conscious Commentary Publishing LLC**

Peace King! Can You Hear Me?
(Poems Inspired by The Love Thy Brotha Day Movement)

Nima Shiningstar-EL

Peace Queen! Can You Hear Me?
(Meditations Inspired by The Love Thy Brotha Day Movement)

Nima Shiningstar-EL

Nabbstract Poetry

Nima Shiningstar-EL

NIMA

Nima Shiningstar-EL

Cosmic Calligraphy   Born Free

Table of Contents

Acknowledgements
Dedication
Introduction

Today is the Day	page 1
Breaking Through	page 4
Dying Empty	page 5
Happy for No Reason	page 6
Boundless	page 7
Hero of the Weirdos	page 8
God is in my Heart	page 9
The Transmission of Light	page 10
Journal Entry #1	page 11
I Build Bridges to the Stars	page 12
Sebi Anti-Toxin	page 13
I Pray that I Get Another Day	page 14
Journal Entry #2	page 15
Horizons of Worship	page 16
Journal Entry #3	page 17
Sitting in Loud Silence	page 18
Regular Words	page 19
Letting it all Melt Away	page 20
Cleanse your Sacred Space	page 21
As Above, So Below	page 22
It's All Inside of You	page 23
I Write God Deadly Venom	page 24
Exorcism	page 25
I Fight Back	page 26
Salvator	page 27
Slightly Different	page 28
You Can Do It…Don't Worry	page 29
A New Apocrypha	page 30
Inner Space	page 31
Grey Jedi Mentality	page 32
Why I "Left"	page 33

Journal Entry #4	page 36
Divine Auras	page 37
When You See a Starship in the Sky	page 38
New Books	page 39
These Words are True	page 40
Writing Out-Loud	page 41
Journal Entry #5	page 42
Participate in Your Life	page 43
Read and Then DO!	page 44
Are You?	page 45
Journal Entry #6	page 46
Life Will Punch You in the Face	page 47
LOS to Born Free (Reflecting)	page 49
Born Free to??? (Visioning)	page 50
You Must Get Over It	page 51
Verzuz	page 53
Just Breathe	page 54
Stop	page 55
One	page 56
Injoy Your life	page 57
Journal Entry #7	page 59
When I Spill	page 60
Anonymous Prophets	page 61
Journal Entry #8	page 62
The Language of Trees	page 63
I Know It's Taking Forever	page 65
Word is Bond	page 66
Separation is Death	page 67
Be Faithful to Yourself	page 68
Too Many Leave Violently	page 70
Journal Entry #9	page 71
Shabbat Shalom	page 72
Journal Entry #10	page 74
God's Got You	page 75
Burdened with Glorious Purpose	page 77
Cosmic Kid	page 78
Excuse My Appearance	page 79
My Ultimate Questions	page 80
Gazing at the Super Moon	page 81
I Begin an End with God	page 82

Cosmic Calligraphy   Born Free

Journal Entry #11	page 83
Love Breaks All Barriers	page 84
Indulgence	page 86
Best Love Ever	page 89
Journal Entry #12	page 90
I'm Overwhelmed by You	page 91
This Ache	page 92
Please Don't Leave my Side	page 93
Winter Solstice	page 94
Universal Architects	page 95
Universal Archeologists	page 96
Universal Frequencies	page 97
Universal Language	page 98
Universal Journey	page 99
Universal Love	page 100
They Are One	page 101
Journal Entry #13	page 102
You Were Born on Purpose	page 103
Cosmic Dust	page 104
It's Survival of the Fittest	page 107
Black Monolith's	page 108
Portals of Prayer	page 110
My Approach	page 111
Journal Entry #14	page 112
Head to the Stars	page 113
My Cosmic Calligraphy	page 114
Without Love, Faith, and Action	page 116
Capricorn One	page 117
Journal Entry #15	page 119
I See Revelation in this Conversation	page 120
Shards of Glass	page 121
Organic Therapeutics	page 123
Interstellar Siddurs	page 124
NINA	page 125
While We	page 126
Ticking Time Bombs	page 127
Toda Raba	page 128
It's More Than One	page 130
Journal Entry #16	page 131
Love Level Vibrational Venting	page 132

Lost in the Space Between Our Ears	page 135
Journal Entry #17	page 138
I Don't Have any Icy Bezels	page 139
I Write Doctrines	page 140
The Streets Don't Care about Black People	page 141
Don't Run from Yourself	page 144
What Scares me the Most	page 145
Everyone Knows	page 146
Connectivity	page 147
Journal Entry #18	page 149
We're Greater	page 150
Ultra-Magnetic	page 151
I Dip My Pen in Blood	page 152
With Each Inscription	page 153
Flat or Round?	page 154
Journal Entry #19	page 157
Stargates	page 158
The Root Chakra (Muladhara)	page 159
Sacral Chakra (Svadhishthana)	page 160
Solar Plexus Chakra (Manipura)	page 161
The Heart Chakra (Anahata)	page 162
The Throat Chakra (Vishuddha)	page 163
The Third Eye Chakra (Ajna)	page 164
The Crown Chakra (Sahasrara)	page 165
Prayers and Meditation Work	page 166
Who or What Guides You	page 167
Sacred Timeline	page 168
Sage and Soldiers	page 172
I Fly Like a Falcon	page 173
What If...	page 174
Journal Entry #20	page 175
Liquid Science	page 176
Sisters of the Valley	page 177
Y'all Can't See Me	page 179
I Can't Turn This Off	page 180
On My Glorious Path Back to God	page 181
Each One of my Books	page 182
I Am the Trend	page 184
Burning the High Table	page 185
Hard Trials	page 187

One Second	page 188
Never Lied in my Verses	page 189
Broadcasting	page 191
51 Years In	page 192
Be Open	page 194
Journal Entry #21	page 195
Some Days	page 196
Love Beckons Us	page 197
You Found Me	page 198
Journal Entry #22	page 199
New Ink…New Design	page 200
Journal Entry #23	page 202
Love Paraphernalia	page 203
Journal Entry #24	page 206
Plant Based Love	page 207
Journal Entry #25	page 210
Be	page 211
The Fountain	page 212
Us Against the World	page 213
Think Beloved, Think!	page 214
Heavy	page 215
All is Not Lost	page 217
I Will	page 218
The Devil Isn't Winning	page 220
The Choice is Yours	page 221
Untraditional	page 224
Get out of God's Way	page 225
Not All	page 228
Don't Listen to Naysayers	page 229
Journal Entry #26	page 230
L' Shana Tova	page 231
Unclassified	page 232
I Wish You Heaven	page 233
Journal Entry #27	page 234
Wake Up, Get Up	page 235
You Won't Always Know the Way	page 236
Journal Entry #28	page 237
The Doer	page 238
Listen	page 240
Stay Loyal	page 241

Cosmic Calligraphy   Born Free

Journal Entry #29   page 242
Close the Gaps   page 243
The Book of Born Free   page 244
From the Bottom of the Rabbit Hole   page 245
Tend to your Garden   page 246
God Told me to Release Them   page 247
Journal Entry #30   page 248
Original People   page 249
Are We Really   page 251
Journal Entry #31   page 252
Penultimate   page 253
This Morning   page 255

Previous Books by Born Free   page 258
Other Books by
Conscious Commentary Publishing   page 259
About Author   page 260

Acknowledgements

Shalom and Toda Raba Almighty God! The Most High! I owe everything to you! The God of Abraham, Isaac, and Jacob, Sarah, Rebecca, Rachel, and Leah! The Supreme Father! The Supreme Mother! The Supreme Everything! Thank you for giving me all my talents and gifts.

For all those who have supported and invested in me, you have my gratitude and appreciation forever and ever! Ya'll keep me going and I absolutely don't take you for granted!

Major love goes to my beautiful and amazing daughter Safiya for being my quality control department on this project. Your eye is next level, and I knew once you gave me your magic co-sign, I knew I was ready to go. Thanks buddy – Love you!

QVision is here!!! Connect @ linktr.ee/Qvisionillustrations

Thanks to Nima for always being my sounding board and inspiring me to be the best! Love and Respect you!!!

Connect and Invest in Nima of NimaGirlProductions @ https://linktr.ee/nimagirlproductions

Salute to my Intelligent Muzik Family. Special embrace to my brothers KUSH and Masada for believing in me and giving me my flowers!

Dedication

I dedicate this book to all my outer and inner cosmic Astronauts, Cosmonauts, Ka Zodiak's, Barbarella's, Prince's, Dirty Computer's, Badu's, Electronica's, Starseeds, Wildseeds, Octavia Butler's, Missy Elliot's, Sun Ra's, Killah Priest's and his Rocketeers, Bjork's, Wangechi Mutu's, Flying Lotus's, Kool Keith's, Jedi's, Afrofuturists, and my Parliament-Funkadelic Afronauts.

Introduction

Cosmic Calligraphy marks my 9th book in 4 years. The math embedded in this understanding is so clear to me. I'm not going to spend a lot of time breaking everything down and writing a long introduction. I just want to say that this book has been one of my favorites to experience and give birth to. In all my work I strive to be as open and honest as humanly possible. I strive to express exactly how I'm feeling and thinking at that moment in my life. Cosmic Calligraphy is no different. In fact, I have gotten more personal and more revealing with this release. I know that some of the ideas that I'm manifesting are not for everyone, and I'm extremely okay with that. I think one of the jobs of a creative, is to shake things up and encourage the audience to experience life from different perspectives.

I have always been a sci-fi fan. Most science fiction TV shows, books, magazines, and films interest me. From Kubrick to Christopher Nolan and so many in-between, traveling through the cosmos, has always been a dream of mine. When I was about 6 ½ my dad took me to see Star Wars: A New Hope. I can't say exactly what happened to me, but I was in total shock and pure wonder and excitement. The idea that the universe is this vast community of life forms engaged in an intergalactic battle for freedom, justice, and equality, pulled me right in. So, as you read this book, you'll see its influence on my mind and spirit. Also, when I was young, I was fascinated with my inner world of thoughts, feelings, emotions, imagination, dreams, and desires. For me, the outer and the inner worlds work hand in hand and are complementary. I think one without the other weakens them both. With this body of work, I'm on a journey inside the layers of all my worlds.

Cosmic Calligraphy							Born Free

I'm just flowing in the moment and not trying to over think what I'm feeling. What you read is what came to my spirit at that appointed time and space. Also, I got out of the way and let Almighty God shine his divine light through me. Whenever I do that, I know everything is going to come out excellent and timeless.

I know what Cosmic Calligraphy means to me but I'm going to let you have your own experience without my overbearing interference. I want you to have your own free and unencumbered journey through my mind and spirit. I have packed in a lot of themes and ideas inside these pages. A lot of what I'm speaking on will go in many different directions, but I pray that the core underlying theme of love, light, and life leaps off the page and connects with your true self.

I sincerely appreciate you for taking the time to invest into me and my thoughts. I pray that we get a chance to connect and continue to build and add on to the progression of love, light, and life!

Thank you once again!

Born Free #therealbornfree

The possible has been tried and failed.
Now it's time to try the impossible.

Sun Ra

Today is the Day

Today is the day
the day you've called for
and ran away from
today is the day
and you cannot un-hear
the sounding of the drum

the alarm is blaring
don't cower like a coward
meet that horrid scream head on
the sunlight is waiting to be devoured

today was created by God
it's your gift to do with as you please
but I beg you
don't try to return it
it contains the cure for every pain and disease

today was born for you
celebrate its joyous birth
it pushed through blood and guts
to remind you of your worth

today is the cosmic crucible
that will burn away all your doubts and indecisions
today has presented you with a key
to release you from the internet's soulless prison

today has brought you everything you desired
and everything you feared
all your old and new excuses are useless
the pitch-black road ahead is clear

Cosmic Calligraphy   Born Free

today is the day
be grateful you received another one
today is different
don't compare it to the other ones

today is the day
and it has cornered you on all paths
today is here to forcefully demand
that you give everything that you have

it requires all your comfort
all your security
all your blood
all your devalued currency
all your Bitcoins
all your stock options
all your Crypto
all your Amazon shoppin
all your knowledge
all your wisdom
all your understanding
all your certainty
all your organs
all your faculties
all your loyalty
all your spiritualty
all your privacy
all your possibilities
all your breath
all your virtual realities
all your confidence
all your lack of confidence
all your submission
all your dominance
all your sex and pleasure
all your time
all your obscurity

Cosmic Calligraphy   Born Free

all your abilities
all your sanity

today is the day
that you finally see exactly who you are
today is waiting to give you
another beautifully horrible scar

today is the day
where your potential meets your practice
today is demanding that you
finally become active

today is the day
when faith meets works
today is telling you to your face
that you can't avoid pain or getting hurt

today is the day
yesterday was cremated
all the old beliefs and facts that you carry
must be updated

today is the day
and you cannot wait for someone else to step up
today is the day to speak and act
or forever shut the fuck up

today is the day
today is the day
today is the day
today is the day
today is the day
today is the day
today is the day
today is the day

Breaking Through

Breaking through
the walls of my old thoughts
peeling away the dead skin
of the old sins I was taught

I know my loved ones
didn't mean to hurt me
but teaching me the same toxic lies
did in fact poison me

and it was the kind of poison
that tasted really sweet
when you're a child
you don't get to choose what to eat

so, at 51 I'm still breaking through
the walls of my old thoughts
peeling away the dead skin
of the old sins I was taught

Dying Empty

I'm dying empty
the devil can't tempt me
no weapon formed
can defeat me

I'm releasing all this poetry
prayers, quotes
thoughts, appeals
every word I wrote

whether it's dope or not dope
it's irrelevant
the function justifies the reproduction
of my testament

all my work is evidence
that I honored my gifts from God
and I told you in Morning Wake Up Calls
I wasn't going to take the best of me to the graveyard

Happy for No Reason

I'm happy for no reason
and that opened the universe to me
nothing happened in particular
I'm just feeling light and free
no explanation
no qualification
no justification
no elaboration
no annotations
no presentation
no interpretation
no substantiation
no illustration
no clarification
I'm just happy for no reason
and that calls for a celebration

Boundless

I am boundless
you are boundless
we are boundless
God is boundless

boundless energy flows
through my melanated organism
I was born in the past
to bring you the futures algorithm
it's about to be a shift
in the paradigms perception
the eye on the back of your dollar
is looking in the wrong direction
it's looking out
when it should be looking within
the earth doesn't move
it's your thoughts that spin
and it's time for humanity
to be reborn again
cuz we can't grasp the understanding
that we're God trapped in colorful animal skins
and

I am boundless
you are boundless
we are boundless
God is boundless

(Repeat until you understand)

Hero of the Weirdos

I am the hero of the weirdos
I don't fit in your one-dimensional boxes
I make love to all colors at once
I laugh at your out of tune responses

I'm strange, freaky
odd, bizarre
the one who can speak to Yahweh
by saying Allahu Akbar

eccentric, surreal
exotic, one of one
I studied with God inside the sun
he told me where all light and life come from

in my original domain
I tapped into the universal membrane
and saw that the past, present, and future
are one in the same

Sun-Ra and The Coltrane's
take me beyond astral planes
anyone who colors inside the lanes
will slowly go insane

under black cosmic rain
I let all the bullshit flow down the drain
anyone who teaches a child to hate themselves
is completely inhumane

the true thoughts that live inside my brain
are not for right now but for right later
and once I accepted my beautiful weirdness
God made me his translator

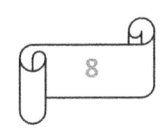

God is in My Heart

God is in my heart
not just my mind
the true power of God
goes beyond how he she's defined

our words are limited
that's why our ancestors used stories
metaphors, myths
symbols, allegories

they wrote them in Horoscopes
the Zodiac is a celestial open book
you were born under the first Heavenly library
lift your head and look

it's all truth
I'm learning how to decode it
if you want to understand original knowledge
study the culture that wrote it

so, study yourself
from your skin tone to your chromosomes
you don't need be Sherlock Holmes
to know that the galaxy is your genome

so, I roam deep inside life's honeycomb
it's the place where I find Shalom
but after I hear the class bell ring
I leave my home inside my home

and go out and live the principles
live the words in my extraterrestrial scripture
cuz once I did the words of 1 John 4:1
became the clearest picture

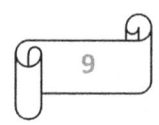

The Transmission of Light

The Transmission of Light
the Integral Vision
The Kabbalah, The Zohar
I conduct original wisdom
The Naked Truth
The Secret Teachings of the Ages
The Wisdom of Solomon and US
is alive in these pages
In the Name of Allah
Man, God, and Civilization
The Dancing Wu-Li Masters
have returned to heal the nation
I revealed my righteous Serpent Power
Christianity before Christ
The Seat of the Soul
melts all winters ice
this is the Universe in a Nutshell
The Science of Self
The Everyman's Talmud
the rebirth of spiritual health
I took the Jedi Code
and the Book of the Sith
turned up the heat
and turned grey in the mix
if you can understand that
you can master the Theology of Time
and identify the Hero with A Thousand Faces
on every mountain that you climb

Journal Entry #1

My sensitivity is a major STRENGTH and SUPERPOWER!

I Build Bridges to the Stars

I build bridges to the stars
slept with Venus on Mars
the path to God is through the heart
not blackholes and quasars

my scriptures are war and peace
historical clashes with the beast
each line combines the minds
of Killah Priest and Dave East

the deceased still speak
too many missions incomplete
I channel like Daniel
so their souls can find relief

I release a few clues
so you can choose or not choose
freedoms voice is choice
it's always been up to you

Sebi Anti-Toxin

I create wormholes
with my frontal lobe
consume globes
in a Unicron wardrobe

in this episode
I launch deep space probes
I'm looking for the cure
for those racist microbes

that have infected, the selected
the broken, the neglected
the naïve, the self-deceived
and the unsuspected

but with the samples I've collected
I've created another Sebi anti-toxin
God's children need more options
than Pfizer, Moderna, and Johnson and Johnson

they need natures remedies
natural amenities
natural melodies
to fight off our natural enemies

Sebi was fulfilling the prophecies
with ancient alkaline policies
his natural earth ideologies
threatened cancerous corporate monopolies

cuz one of our greatest commodities
is the Sebi anti-toxin
cuz God's children need more options
than Pfizer, Moderna, and Johnson and Johnson

I Pray that I Get Another Day

I pray that I get another day
I have a few more things to say
a few more blank pages
for me to display

all my words and talent
the colors on my palette
I've tried to be a good man
I pray my efforts were valid

I've fallen short many times
covered up my sins inside rhymes
my crimes seeped into my vines
and now you can taste it in my wine

but I pray that I get another day
I have a few more things to say
I still have a few more blank pages
for me to confess and convey

Journal Entry #2

The impossible
becomes instantly possible
when you believe in yourself
and you activate
your limitless potential

Horizons of Worship

Flying through
horizons of worship
in my peaceful warship
God made sure I'm fully equipped

with original Hebrew Bibles
weapons for survival
adamantium hammers
to destroy false idols

in this new cycle
we made a religion out of denial
so the work that we're doing
is vital

it's time to revisit Ethiopia
the Tigray Region
where you must make a climb of faith
to receive the ancient teachin

the frescoes painted in the chapels in the sky
will resonate with your third eye
and those who take the narrow path
will never truly die

when you enter the horizons of worship
remove your shoes and daily disguises
for you are in the Holy presence
of what your journey to God symbolizes

Journal Entry #3

I was never missing

you were just looking for me
in all the wrong places

Sitting in Loud Silence

Sitting in loud silence

my lips are closed so I can converse
my eyes can often write
my best freestyle verse
when you see me sitting there
quietly and slowing breathing with the flowers
just know that I'm with the universal soul
laughing, flying, and talking for hours

Regular Words

These are regular words
but the meaning is subterranean
I was a child of God
before I was a Pennsylvanian
some say I'm an alien
cuz of the thoughts in my cranium
I just know the difference between
Eddie Kendricks and Eddie Arkadian

Letting it all Melt Away

I'm letting it all melt away
I'm not holding on to anything
that doesn't serve my spirit

I'm letting it all melt away
I'm not thinking about anything
that would rob me of the Heaven left for me to inherit

Cleanse your Sacred Space

Cleanse your sacred space
burning sage is just one step
purge all negative thinking
feel the positive energy flow with each breath

submerge in a Mikvah
until you feel as light as a feather
remember that it is the spirit and not the body
that holds everything together

remove all destructive people from your life
don't let them compromise your health
too much stress
can permanently damage your cells

pray and mediate daily
to keep all your energy gates open
investing in your emotional and spiritual wellbeing
is how you remain unbroken

As Above, So Below

As above, so below
what you reap, you sowed
when you water the universal Tree of Life
all humanity grows

the roots are tangible
and they are spiritual
they are completely factual
and mysteriously allegorical

you can touch each leaf
and eat all its fruit
it equally accepts the divine
and the destitute

be not afraid
we all emerge from the Ein Sof
God listens when we make the sacred oath
but checks our bodies to record the proof of our growth

It's All Inside of You

Whatever you can see
inside your mind's eye
you can manifest in your waking life
you were born
with the natural ability
to take flight

you are more amazing
and more astounding
than you think
God has blessed you
with the inner power
to pull yourself back from the brink

it's all inside of you
you're not lacking
or deficient in anyway
it's all inside of you
God lives inside you
and he will guide you to a brand-new day

I Write God Deadly Venom

I write God deadly venom
to hell I'm sendin them
wild like a young Eminem
on pills and synonyms

from the tribe of Benjamin
my medicine is melanin
don't ever question the roots
of my adrenaline

Vibranium skeleton
survived the pits pendulum
no verbal gelatin
enters my specimen

studied Ms. Gwendolyn
reversed the conditionin
now go tell the children
about the return of God you're witnessin

Exorcism

Spark the incense
the ceremony is intense
when you walk with God
you can't straddle the fence

let's commence with the exorcism
righteous mysticism
I come from the tradition
that says your actions are your religion

it's all narcissism
if you point to the solar system
just to avoid
western barbarism

bring in the women
they're the healers of victims
cuz you can't have your knowledge
without your wisdom

and when they join palms
you feel immediately calm
it's death to your inner
and outer demon spawns

the exorcism at dawn
paved the way for your resurrection
the universal love connection
will be your new protection

I Fight Back

I fight back

physical, mental, and spiritual
my warnings are lyrical
but my actions are undeniable
and karmically justifiable
because you were told in advance
I love everybody
and that's why I give more than one chance
to rethink
and reassess
because if I must take it there
I will leave nothing but a mess
and these are far from threats
and I'm not upset
but if you come at me with blatant disrespect
you will walk away with pain and regret

Salvator

The Salvator Mundi
450 mil was the fetching price
it's a fake beloved
the image is about twenty shades too light
the first earthly image of The Christ
has a deep melanin pigment
this so-called lost da Vinci
is nothing but a greedy soul's figment
of the mind
and slick as shit marketing
the naïve and graven
is who they were targeting
it's disheartening to see
humanity still trying to buy the supreme light
when the true picture of The Christ
is manifested in the conscious actions of your daily life

Slightly Different

What happened to Moses, David, and Yeshua
won't exactly happen to me and mine
we were given different signs
and we live at and in completely different times

when I read the ancient history
I see the futuristic possibilities
but I must be more asymmetrical
than the dark heart of our true enemy

wolves wear more than sheep's clothing
they wear a lot of angel wings
they might have on beads and Ankh's
and not golden calf rings

so, I must be careful
things might come at me in a slightly different way
so, I'm never rigid in my thinking
when dealing with my inner and outer devil's today

You Can Do It...Don't Worry

You can do it
you can stand alone
when you talk and walk with God
you are never alone

and don't worry about
letting go of people
who have already
let go of you

I will say that again

don't worry about
letting go of people
who have already
let go of you

YOU CAN DO IT!
DON'T WORRY!
YOU CAN DO IT!
DON'T WORRY!
YOU CAN DO IT!
DON'T WORRY!
YOU CAN DO IT!
DON'T WORRY!
YOU CAN DO IT!
DON'T WORRY!
YOU CAN DO IT!
DON'T WORRY!
YOU CAN DO IT!
DON'T WORRY!
YOU CAN DO IT!
DON'T WORRY!

A New Apocrypha

I birthed a new Apocrypha
vivid like solar photographers
I first emerged
from the womb of Andromeda

I speak the unpopular
my degrees are keys
please reread
the 1st and 2nd Maccabees

get off your knees
try to see what I see
waterproof papyrus
pulled from the Dead Sea

it's me Born Free
the bookstore carnivore
I was there for
Genesis 5:24

I'm no longer unsure
I see the tunnel beyond the light
I regained my sight
after years in carbonite

every line that I write
comes from my sacred space
read Psalm 78:68
to get a quick taste

Inner Space

Outer space
is not the final frontier
our greatest journey
will begin and end right here

the depth of the human heart
cannot be fully quantified or measured
our voyage through inner space
is where we'll find life's most profound treasures

Grey Jedi Mentality

I have a grey Jedi mentality
a balanced spiritual anatomy
but some believe that I'm flirting
with tragedy and catastrophe

I understand their concerns
play with fire and you'll fly with Icarus
but if I never go near the fire
how will I burn away my ignorance

I'm more Qui-Gon
than Obi-Won
I'm really both
on a balancing beam is where I took my oath

you can become one with the force
and still have deep personal connections
the force isn't the Jedi's
or the Sith's sole possession

Why I "Left"

I didn't leave this earth
to run away
I "left"
to prevent our doomsday

Almighty God has given us
millions of people and billboards
to warn us
about his double edge sword

Almighty God has given us
millions of chances to choose a better tomorrow
he has given us every opportunity
to avoid these preventable sorrows

but we're choosing
to die senselessly in this global crib
humanity is vanity
we don't know how to live

we refuse to give
what Almighty God has given to all of us
life, love, warmth, patience,
friendship, forgiveness, imagination, and trust

we seem to lust for the dry dust
we seem to desire hell fire
so, I came out here
to get reinspired

Cosmic Calligraphy   Born Free

I came out here
to silence the gunfire
I came out here
because all our efforts have backfired

I came out here
to re-learn how to vibrate higher
I came out here
to re-embrace my passion and desire

I came out here
to find my missing smile and laughter
I came out here
to start my next chapter

I came out here
to refill my tires
I came out here
to reattach my wires

cuz we're about to expire
hopefully, I can find the intergalactic Rosetta Stone
I came out here
to save our home

I came out here
to find a cure for our stupidity syndrome
because our collective actions
have us marching into a FEMA biodome

I came out here
because I know we can be better
but I'm still afraid
that it's going to take
more senseless death
to bring us closer together

Cosmic Calligraphy   Born Free

I'm on my way back
I learned a lot from my outer and inner quest
my screen and my soul
has been refreshed

I'm coming through the atmosphere
I can see that the spirit of death is still here
but no worries
I've brought back the cure to defeat fear

I'm ready this time
the sun will shine
I'm ready this time
I have the third temples design

Journal Entry #4

I can't apologize
for being me
I won't apologize
for loving who I love
I can't apologize
for what you don't understand
I won't apologize
for what you can't see or feel
I can't apologize
for your anger and spite
I won't apologize
for joining the fight
I can't apologize
for your misinterpretation
I won't apologize
for my chosen path to salvation

Divine Auras

Shalom Ahki's

we move in divine auras
we ignite our Menorah's
by living The Torah

ancient explorers
my daughter is the legend of Korra
I sat with Muhammad in the cave
when he made the first Surah

it was so euphoric
allegoric, historic
we entered the coliseum
on Arabian horses

my whole regalia
spiritual paraphernalia
I embody James Baldwin
not Norman Mailer

God is my tailor
I build with Tim Taylor
if you glorify your jailer
you're a mother fuckin failure

flow like Masonic sailor's
gun smoke chokes inhalers
I wrote this for the braillers
and this is just the trailer

When You See a Starship in the Sky

When you see a starship in the sky
just know that they are not visiting
they are coming home
inside the first star born
sleeps our ancestors
oldest bones

New Books

I write new books
every time I speak
the ripple effect is like
fish skippin across cosmic creeks
each draft is a sneak peak
of the new books after Revelations
I'm writing a new chapter of plagues
for the demons that whipped the Haitians

These Words are True

I love you

these words are true
can't won't don't stop
my spirit is renewed

my point of view
is the true and living Creator
you're either love thy neighbor
or a space invader

I spoke at the last Seder
condemned the idol makers
taught my seed and her friends
how to build their own sabers

how to buy more acres
stack more paper
and how to stop the devil from building a nation
on the back of their enslaved labor

Writing Out-Loud

I have always wondered about

where I was before I was here
where is that place located
was I even and I

as I get older
I wonder about where I am going
I would be hurt if this place
was my last stop

Journal Entry #5

Everyday it's possible
don't submit to the obstacle
when you believe in yourself
you become unstoppable
these times are volatile
in bad ways and good
once you accept this reality
the visions you see will be understood

Participate in Your Life

Participate in your life
get motivated about your dreams
invest in your ideas
be your own team

don't wait for the approval
move with urgency
don't worry about the money
your energy creates currency

be your own hype man
your own hype woman
make yourself go viral
keep pushin, keep pushin

don't wait until the morning
start your mission tonight
nothing will work right
until you, participate in your life

Read and Then DO!

Read and then do

this is how all spirits get through
study and study hard
study your trade, study God
but after you finish studying
all the words on the page
close that damn book
get up and become fully engaged

Are You?

Are you Thomas Anderson
or are you Neo
are you the Oracle
or are you Miss Cleo

the difference between the two
is as stark as life and death
Battle Cat or Cringer
your first or last breath

life's true depth
can't be perceived from the fringes
just like you can't find true enlightenment
through Fentanyl lenes

life's game is a game of inches
no time for wallowing
how many white rabbits are you following
verses how many blue pills are you're swallowing

Journal Entry #6

I wasn't ignoring you
you were calling me
by the wrong name

Life Will Punch You in the Face

Once you accept
that life will punch you in the face
you'll be ready
to get back in life's race

most of us try to avoid
getting hit at all
that's why we don't try anything
that might make us fall

but what you don't realize
or haven't fully embraced
is that everyone that is successful
has been punched multiple times in the face

they have been betrayed
they have been viciously kicked
they have been lied on
and treated less than shit

but that didn't stop them
from getting back in the ring
they go back into their fighting stance
ready for the next fight that life brings

so, take a deep breath
and watch out for the left
and most times the right
your face will get touched tonight

but don't let that stop you
from raising the stakes
don't be afraid to find out
how salty your blood tastes

Cosmic Calligraphy   Born Free

cuz it's going to be okay beloved
you will survive
and you'll finally discover
what it means to be truly alive

cuz none of my blessings would be possible
and I would have never become great
if I did put myself in the uncomfortable position
to get punched in the face

LOS to Born Free (Reflecting)

I went from LOS to Born Free
but the transition wasn't seamless
my heart felt genius kept getting bullied
by the arrogance of my penis

I was never the meanest
overall, my history is kind
but being intelligently deaf, dumb, and blind
kept me so far behind

I read a thousand books
but I didn't take a thousand steps
when you read more than you live
you'll never be ready for what's next

but I can say today
I'm more Born Free than ever before
and God just told me that he
unlocked the bottom lock on his front door

I know everything isn't instantly forgiven
just because of my new admissions
but my old cancer of consciousness
is finally in remission

so, I can say today
I'm more Born Free than ever before
and God just told me that he
left open his front door

Born Free to??? (Visioning)

Now that I'm Born Free
I'm excited about my next evolution
cuz having knowledge of self
is not the conclusion

studying my Torah
and the science of everything in life
is not the final path
towards everlasting life

becoming one with the one God
might take me more than three score and ten
I'm trying to do as much as I can
so I don't have to come back again

but since I started late
and spend too many years lost in dumb debates
getting everything that I want
might have to wait

but on a lighter note
Born Free is the best version of me
I'm a better father, mate, and friend
with God's light shining through me

as Born Free, my possibilities are endless
I'm excited about my next evolution
cuz having a deep knowledge of self
is not my spirits conclusion

You Must Get Over It

You must get over it
I know that sounds callous, heartless, and mean
especially if you lost someone
or have been through something equally extreme

give me a chance to explain
give me a chance to smooth out the edges
give me a chance to pull this reckless thought
back in from the narrow ledges

I'm not talking about overnight
or even over hundred nights
but at some point
you must move on with your life

and while I'm saying this of you
I'm looking right in the soul of my mirror
cuz I've been my personal pains
main cheerleader and torchbearer

so I know how hard it is
to let go of what hurts you the most
but you must untie yourself
from the whipping post

as each day passes, I see
more than the weather changing
all kinds of relationships
going through bitter cycles of rearranging

I lost my brother
God, please bless and rest his soul
I've fallen deep in depressions hole
feeling defeated and out of control

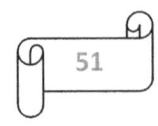

Cosmic Calligraphy   Born Free

for me, death is the hardest
wound to close up
it's the only thing that ever
made me not want to wake up

pain is a son of a bitch
depression is a mother fucka
and that's why I'm adamant
that we must love and help each other

so, I'm not saying get over it
like you can forget the tragedies that happened
I guess what I'm trying to say is that we must
find a way to live with the tragedies that happened

this kind of advice can sound clear to the brain
but insane to the broken heart
and because of that
it feels impossible to make a fresh start

I hope I'm not fucking up this message
or minimizing your hurt
the last thing I want to do
is to act like dealing with grief is easy work

beloved, I know how deep wounds can go
and I don't want to sound like an insensitive hypocrite
but to truly heal
we ALL must find a way to get up and get over it

Verzuz

Yeah, I love Verzuz

Kane Verzuz Kris
but it's the Verzuz within self
that causes me to flip

sometimes I'm LOX Verzuz Dip
total annihilation
other times I'm Jill Verzuz Erykah
pure unification

self-salvation
is self-savior
losing the Verzuz within self
is what turned Anakin into Vader

it's what turned W'Kabi
against Okoye
the Verzuz within self
must be fought and won everyday

Just Breathe

Just breathe
and believe in yourself
just breathe
and believe in yourself
just breathe
and believe in yourself
just breathe
and believe in yourself
just breathe
and believe in yourself
just breathe
and believe in yourself
just breathe
believe in yourself
just breathe
and believe in yourself
just breathe
and believe in yourself
just breathe
and believe in yourself
just breathe
and believe in yourself
just breathe
and believe in yourself

Stop

Stop fighting against
your own best interest
so many things can change
if you just look at it different

stop putting bullets
in your enemy's gun
when you stop arguing with ignorance
you already won

stop lying to yourself
face the truth about yourself and others
some people are not worthy
to be your sister and brother

stop running from your dreams
accept that nothing will be easy
once you accept that you can't escape pain or injury
God will deliver to you your greatest victory

One

We've given the Creator a trillion names
he answers us in every twisted tongue
and we still can't understand
how The Most-High is just one

Adonai still loves us
even though we can't grasp that Allah is all
if we just understood this one reality
we might stop humanities next fall

Injoy Your life

Injoy your life
knowledge and fun
are NOT mutually exclusive
don't let your intellect
turn you into
a disagreeable reclusive

don't spend too many days
talking about how things
are fucked up and bad
be grateful about the sunshine
and good times
you've been blessed to have

now before you
give me the side eye
I'm not dismissing
your pain and suffering
I'm not saying that
your broken heart
comes from nothing

but I AM saying
that destruction
isn't the only prophesy revealed
anger and sorrow
aren't the only things
that your heart and soul can feel

because I know
depression is real
and it can come down
on you like a hammer

Cosmic Calligraphy					Born Free

so, while you're speaking
your divine word
balance out your grammar

injoy your life
knowledge and fun
are NOT mutually exclusive
don't let your intellect
turn you into
a disagreeable and lonely reclusive

Journal Entry #7

Commitment
makes your blueprint relevant
commitment
extends all relationships
commitment
gives you full admittance
commitment
gives your legacy permanence

When I Spill

When I spill
it's like how twenty-four scientists build
I drop to stop
the next Christ from being killed
my truth is sealed
in the Torah scrolls of old
I arose in God's city
where the roads are paved in gold
I compose and transmit
calligraphy and Sanskrit
cuz all this nigga shit
is fuckin rancid
I've been rebranded
Son of Man, Sun of God
my words hit hard
like Elijah's answers to Fard

Anonymous Prophets

I'm one of the anonymous prophets
that write sacred documents
that inspire the populace
to end the devil's dominance
I'm seeding every continent
with God's true consciousness
cuz what we have now
is idolatrous
we have more opulence
a virtual metropolis
but when it comes to basic humanity
we channel Remus and Romulus
I don't believe in coincidence
everything is providence
and if we don't turn towards love and life
we'll suffer Revelation's consequence

Journal Entry #8

Some say as a man thinketh
I say as a man doeth
your actions confirm
if your thoughts are the truest

The Language of Trees

Trees speak
beyond our concept of sound
trees link
roots holding hands underground

they feed each other
subterranean networks
they can heal each other
they're nursed by mother earth

they give and receive
help us all breathe
the same lines on the palms of your hands
mirror the lines on the face of all leaves

their ecosystem
eclipses are egoism
they thrive through collectivism
and we die because of separatism

our narcissism
distorts our hearing
trees are constantly speaking to us
giving us medicine for healing

from cool shade to maple syrup
our homes and our books
good mental health
and fresh herbs to cook

trees give us so much
but what do we give back to them
they have never been our enemies
but we don't treat them as friends

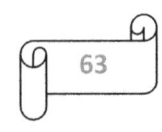

Cosmic Calligraphy   Born Free

only a few can comprehend
the relationships between trees
the friendships grown in the forests
last beyond centuries

we must accept the clear reality
that we aren't the only conscious beings
trees know and understand
trees have feelings

trees feel sensations
from their crowns down through their foundations
photosynthesis shows us
trees connecting through solar vibrations

trees are having conversations
on all occasions
through every generation
they enhance all populations

it's our natural obligation
to start policing the fleecing
I don't think we really overstand
the hell on earth we're unleashing

but as our knowledge is increasing
we can understand trees deeper meaning
and teach our children the reason
why our death cycle must stop repeating

I know this is revealing
and commercially unappealing
but if we don't listen to the language of trees
humanity will continue rotting and reeling

I Know It's Taking Forever

I know it's taking forever
but keep your feet moving
stay focused beloved
God knows what he's doing
I know it's uncomfortable
but keep flying higher
take your hands off the wheel
God is the best driver

Word is Bond

Word is bond
the legacy, I carry on
you subscribe to black death
downloaded on Patreon
exclusive nigga shit
blood money memberships
I prayed during the last eclipse
that God brings the apocalypse
this system can't be fixed
we need the fire this time
can't say it any clearer
cuz all our problems don't rhyme
what happens to us
happens to all of humankind
seek and ye shall find
Matthew 13:39

Separation is Death

Separation is death
this message is a warning
together is the only way
we all see a bright new morning

we all say
we want a better day
and then we argue about the means
and kill each other with no delay

God gave us all
a piece of the puzzle
we were supposed to put them together
to raise humanity from the rubble

but if we continue
down this divergent path
nothing we create
will last

if we continue
using politics, economics, religion, music,
the internet, science, art, and the military as weapons
we will never answer
life's most eternal questions

because separation is death
this message is a warning
together is the only way
we all see a bright new morning

Be Faithful to Yourself

Be faithful to yourself

activate your plans
don't wait until your family
and friends understand

don't foolishly wait decades
like I did
don't wait until God
begins to close your eyelids

don't focus on the outcome
or if "they" say you look like a clown
be faithful to yourself
get your shit off the ground

don't compare yourself to the next
like I did
what kind of legacy
are you leaving for your kids

be faithful to yourself
have your own back
focus on what you have
don't worry about what you lack

as long as you keep it moving
God will provide
believing in yourself
is how all dreams stay alive

I played
a very foolish game
I almost fucked around
and extinguished my own flame

I gave everyone around me
all that I had
and when it came time for me
I had very little left in my bag

so, please feel me when I say

be faithful to yourself
activate your plans
don't wait until your family
and friends understand

don't foolishly wait decades
like I did
don't wait until God
begins to close your eyelids

Too Many Leave Violently

Too many leave violently
over savage economy's
they graduated from school
with diplomas and lobotomies

no equality
no sanity
they murder best friends
over IG vanity

the gravity of ignorance
is punishing and crushing
they're all John Snow's
they know absolutely nothing

the devil ain't bluffin
young blood is gushin
God is yelling, stop praying
get up and do something!

the pain is mounting
the angels are shouting
our indifference to black death
is astounding

compounding each story
is a vain attempt at internet glory
toe tagged potential dads
forgotten in unnamed categories

Journal Entry #9

Hypocrisy has always been
one of humanities most consistent philosophies
do as I say and not as I do
has always been the policy
I don't know if it's by nature or nurture
the end game is always the same
our hearts have a different face
from the one we openly claim

Shabbat Shalom

Shabbat Shalom
I'm still in the zone
I take this more serious
than just a poem

rock from planet to planet
new star to star
I tear it up y'all
I've been blessed by God

I carve mosaics
odd phrases forgotten native
I shun hatred
a young elder in the Matrix

my greatness is sacred
each statement took patience
my pen is blazin
cuz I'm never complacent

I'm not a Mason
but I square my compass
give solace to the novice
put the rest in hospice

I hate pompous vomit
these demonic topics
fake symbolic prophets
here to rape our wallets

Cosmic Calligraphy   Born Free

they take God's knowledge
and mix Lucifer's logic
digitally toxic
to increase their profits

devils stop it
fuck the Tik-Tok gossip
all my sonnets
fulfill God's promise

Journal Entry #10

Without a relationship
with God and yourself
your relationship with others
will be unnecessarily challenging

God's Got You

God's got you
don't worry about the sidelines
God's got you
don't keep looking behind
God's got you
don't doubt or despair
God's got you
he's always there

they will come after you
they will resurrect the old you
to destroy the new you
but don't worry, cuz God's got you

they will bear false witness
try to infect you with their spiritual sickness
but if you lean on God
she will heal you with the quickness
cuz

God's got you
don't worry about the sidelines
God's got you
don't keep looking behind
God's got you
don't doubt or despair
God's got you
he's always there

prioritize your mental health
prioritize your emotional health
prioritize your spiritual health
prioritize your physical health

if those you know or knew
can't handle your renewal
don't waste any time
trying to get their approval
cuz

God's got you
don't worry about the sidelines
God's got you
don't keep looking behind
God's got you
don't doubt or despair
God's got you
he's always there

I know that everybody won't understand me
I accept it
everybody won't support me
I accept it
everybody won't like or love me
I accept it
everybody won't want or need me
I accept it

and if those you know or knew
can't handle your renewal
don't waste any time
trying to get their approval
cuz

God's got you
don't worry about the sidelines
God's got you
don't keep looking behind
God's got you
don't doubt or despair
God's got you
he's always there

Burdened with Glorious Purpose

Burdened with glorious purpose
don't interpret God's servant
your soul's been seduced
by the serpent

I move in a warm current
updating old sermons
sippin aged bourbon
putting hedges around virgins

vermin are always lurkin
death behind the curtain
but we can realign the timeline
and change the predetermined

my mind is always workin
cuz my soul is always yearnin
for the fires set by men
to finally stop burning

Cosmic Kid

I've always been
a cosmic kid
ethereal thoughts
surrounded my crib

I used all sixty-four crayons
at the same time
I tagged the walls
with an intelligent design

my young body
radiated intense heat
I first started time traveling
in my sleep

I visited first world Synagogues
Churches and Masjid's
my dreams always lived
off this earthly grid

I stood amid the reality of street life
and the passion of the Hebrew Christ
my spirit took flight
beyond Dagobah heights

what I write today
is a part of my prophecy
but before I can see the vastness of this galaxy
I must understand and love my inner odyssey

Excuse My Appearance

Excuse my appearance
but God is working on my substance
I'm sorry for my disappearance
but God gave me my abundance

I am not who I was
I am not who you say I am
I was never as pure as the lamb
I've failed hundreds of his exams

I used to speak ham
and barbeque the spam
I was more like the Son of Sam
and less like the seed of Abraham

but as I grew as a man
I've gone farther as a father
one tried to tarnish my honor
I just shrugged and didn't bother

I prosper as the author
to write my new legacy
I see the face of eternity
cuz I keep God's path in front of me

so, **e**xcuse my appearance
but God is working on my substance
I'm sorry for my disappearance
but God gave me my abundance

My Ultimate Questions

My ultimate questions
aren't about the depth of the mind
I wonder more about why humanity
struggles so hard to be kind

not individually
but in our collective expression
why can't we learn from history's
bloodiest lessons

thinking about our thoughts is important
studying consciousness is critical
but the fact that we cannot stop
hurting each other is regretful and pitiful

why is it so hard for us to give
and so easy for us to take
what's the value of a theory of everything
if our love keeps getting murdered by our hate

Gazing at the Super Moon

Gazing at the super moon
I feel myself starting to swoon
I can hear our ancestors speak
we are forever attuned

we have Zoom group chats
without artificial devices
the connection is more than beneficial
it is priceless

they take me through Quantum gateways
and over subatomic bridges
they showed me the riverbank
where Yeshua gathered his first fishes

I saw all the other versions
of me and my family
they told me the secrets
of restoring my vitality

each of their voices
rises and harmonizes
sometimes they lovingly critique
other times they lovingly advise

this spiritual exercise
always happens when the moon gets closer
I love when I feel our ancestors
lovingly tapping on my shoulders

I Begin an End with God

I begin and end with God
to keep meaning in the equation
without God as the Alpha and Omega
I lose all interest in the calculation

I travel to places
where my science friends deny
they hang they're hat on the when, where, and how
I get into bed with the why

and since science creates reasons
for everything we do and discuss
God has his reason for why
he created us

this is my path
this keeps me happy on my search
my laboratory has always been in the attic
of a Synagogue, Temple, Garden, and highest perch

Journal Entry #11

You can't love in half measures
or with small droplets of rain
you must love with the force of a thousand tsunami's
to wash away your hearts pain

Love Breaks All Barriers

Love breaks all barriers
love is not bound by any clocks
love translates in all languages
love is a force that cannot be stopped

we love our children
before they draw their first breath
this is the kind of love
that gives purpose to our steps

we love our loved ones
after they die
this is the kind of love
that only intensifies

love covers the entire spectrum
don't try to give it a single definition
love doesn't share
our manufactured inhibitions

love can be clearly observed
but not rigidly measured
love is what
keeps us tethered

love cannot be locked in
or be forced to walk in our shallow regiments
love doesn't want to be bothered
with our petty prejudice

Cosmic Calligraphy   Born Free

beloved, if we are to ever
overcome our man-made conflicts
love must be the primary part
of the fix

if we are to ever
journey to other star systems
universal love
must accompany us on the mission

love comes in forms
that are subtle and unsuspecting
love is one of the key gifts from God
that we better start respecting

love is the absence of confusion
love shatters all illusions
love filters out our human pollution
love solidifies our evolution

because love breaks all barriers
love is not bound by any clocks
love translates in all languages
love is a force that cannot be stopped

Indulgence

We're beyond indulgence
beyond reluctance
we drank each other's
pure cane substance

our eyes turned yellow
our skin got darker
and then we violently ripped off
all our armor

now we're bloody and naked
completely unprotected
the feelings that came next
were so unexpected

both our organs swelled
and became erected
new husband and wife
no longer neglected

and once we disconnected
from this earth's erosion
we found the flower power
of love's true explosion

the force of the blast
destroyed our past
now we're free at last
free at last

Cosmic Calligraphy   Born Free

planets fell out of orbit
we forgot our torment
it's always godsent
when you get a chance to reinvent

sometimes old memories
can murder your new remedies
we got rid of those old accessories
so we can dance freely in our new treasury

this energy is extraterrestrial
our view is aerial
we no longer participate
in hate's disrespectful burials

we entered each other
we are one
all our old names and categories
are done

we contain all we need
we both lead
when we're both hungry
we look within and feed

we are no longer we
androgyny is God's true nature
inside God
all otherness disappears in the vapor

so, don't look for me
in he or she
just embrace
our totality

because I am happy
I am happy
I am happy
I am happy
I am happy
I am happy
I am happy
I am happy

Best Love Ever

This is the best love ever
because I want and need you
and you want and need me
at the same exact time

Journal Entry #12

Love doesn't want you to perform for her
your love should be as natural as breathing
when love see's someone putting on a big show
she knows the performer and performance is deceiving

I'm Overwhelmed by You

I'm overwhelmed by you
crushed under the weight of everything I desire
I willingly submit to the engagement
that your eyes subtly conspire
I've tried to be strong
but my love for you breaks all agreements
my strength has secretly
made a covenant with my weakness
they are working together
so that love's will be done
they learned from the last eclipse
that the sun and moon are naturally one
love has won
love is Almighty God's truest vaccine
given to inoculate our souls
from the doubt that lays eggs in our dreams

you are more than what you seem
your chestnut covering hides a deeper mystery
I wonder if I'm worthy
of such a providential victory
hold me tight inside your liberty
do not let a whisp of air past between
our united love will guarantee
that our pastures will forever remain green
if we pour into each other
what Almighty God gave us in our mother's womb
our love's flesh will never
see the inside of a man's tomb
we are flying through the door my love
our nudity will repel any attack
our eyes, minds, and hearts are fixed on forever
cuz only the fearful and foolish look back

This Ache

This ache is equal parts
life and death
this ache is hungry
it feeds on my breath
the thought of you punishes me
it beats me with the sweetest of all rods
each blow feels like a prayer
straight from the mouth of God
this ache cuts me deep
until my blood runs and dances in the fresh air
it hoists me up on the rack
until all my true feelings are laid bare
I love you beyond
all things known and unknown
if not for this unbearable ache
I would have never found my way back to our home
our sex is next level
each stroke breaks the grip of the devil
and when we cum
we carry loves messages inside each blood vessel
and I love you beyond
all things known and unknown
if not for this unbearable ache
I would have never found my way back to our home

Please Don't Leave my Side

Please don't leave my side
linger until our passion retires for the day
I am not ready to walk away from
Heaven's gateway

the time that we spend together
frees us from time's prison
our love and lust have multiplied
we do not sow to division

come back into my arms
and let me continue to caress your immortality
I promise to restore
all your wet vitality

forsake all former commitments
be not bound to anything outside this tender haven
God will forgive you
he knows that our love is salvation

Winter Solstice

It's the Winter Solstice
beloved, you're gorgeous
our names are written
on the shell of the world tortoise
we made it through the dark forest
feelings no longer dominant
God yelled, hold still
as he painted our portrait

Universal Architects

Universal architects
grand builders of life
grantors of sight
ignitors of light
they don't build edifices
to astound the physical eyes of men
they develop the inner mansion
to house the expression of God within
we each contain a holy ember
but it must be carefully encouraged to grow
we are each responsible
to maintain its omnipresent glow
but without these divine designers
your home of self would fall to disrepair
and you might not ever know
that the true and living God lives there

Universal Archeologists

Universal archeologists
seekers of the ultimate endeavor
they leave their shovels and maps at home
and dig inside our thoughts for original treasures
they break through the concrete of intolerance
the topsoil of hatred
the bedrock of bitterness
to find what's sacred
back when your mind was naked
before it was buried under worldly burdens
before it was uncertain
cowering behind virtual curtains
they excavate to elevate
study the soul to illuminate
if you're an Indiana Jones, go home
your tribe has died trying to foolishly translate

Universal Frequencies

Universal frequencies
6 tones, Solfeggio
don't ask me any questions
if you know you know
the harmony of the spheres
COLTRANE'S Transition
SUN-RA's ARKESTRA
is how all life was christened
in the beginning was the word
and those words were sounds
God's utterance planted seeds
in every multi-versal ground
when we plug into universal frequencies
we see all possibilities
and the best way to absorb that energy
is slowly and deeply

Universal Language

Universal language
we share a common tongue
a smile is understood
everywhere and by everyone
joy and pain
are universally relatable emotions
they are felt by all souls
on all sides of the ocean
my promotion isn't about
the globe using the exact same dialect
I'm not trying to bring
the Tower of Babel back in effect
I want us to connect
a common denominator can be discovered
cuz what's the point of all these devices
if we can't honestly speak and listen to each other

Universal Journey

Universal journey
we're all on a trek
we're all trying to figure out
the meaning of each step
we want to know if this is it
or is there more wonder in store
do we go outside or inside
to find the door
it's no easy path
for the rich or the poor
the mandate for every journey
is to endure
I've tapped into my core
have you done the same
I received more messages and blessings
once I plugged directly into God's mainframe

Universal Love

Universal love
is the key to unlocking Heaven on earth
universal love
embraces every child at birth
if we want global healing
and global survival
we must stop killing
our enemies and rivals
even when you're in the right
taking a life is catastrophic
even when it must be done
it still feeds the hunger of the demonic
this difficult topic
isn't about kumbaya and diversity bullshit
universal love is one of the ladders
we can use to climb out of the devil's pit

They Are One

I am
the Morpheus
of the Mobius Strip
don't trip
science and spirituality
share a fellowship

the Tree of Life
and Kabbalah
are compatible with Einstein
the Metu Neter
the Code of Hammurabi
can speak to Hawking's mind

I've added the Corpus Hermeticum
and the Theory of Relativity
to my wheelhouse
if we combine
the disciplines
we will discover what life is all about

commit to this understanding
swear an oath
to this truth
once we merge science and spirituality
the fruit will end
most of the world's bloodiest disputes

Journal Entry #13

I always repent

that's how I reversed my descent
and then my actions
became the real cement
then I was welcomed back
in Jethro's tent
now I understand what
Acts 3:19 really meant

You Were Born on Purpose

You were born on purpose
don't believe the heresy
your life is the result
of a divine conspiracy
between your mother, your father
and The Most High
and his blessing are upon you
beyond the day that you physically die

Cosmic Dust

I smoke cosmic dust
to get that rush
open my heart
and pull out my paint brush

as my life force begins to gush
I merge with the horizon
meteoric mushrooms
are so mesmerizing

I flew through Orion
created a new calendar for unborn Mayans
that will give them the exact date
when death will stop dying

I got silent when I landed
on MDMA
erotic education
was the lesson of the day

the atmosphere was DMT
they instantly recognized me
all the inhabitants stamped their tongues
with rainbow LSD

we didn't talk with words
but I understood them, and they understood me
we communicated
in the interplanetary slang of PCP

they didn't want me to leave
weed trees grow in abundance
they are IN-tune with the
universal substance of oneness

it's wonderous
they helped me fix my earthly compass
they said all our clocks are wrong
because we've become sunless

the human soul has no circumference
in all directions it roams
touch your 6th Chakra 7 times
if I ever want to go back home

they gave me an emerald brownie
and a small purple cookie
they could sense
that I wasn't a rookie

the Watchers were watching
as I became a Doula in a Nephilim birth
this used to happen all the time
back when we had an Alkaline earth

our spiritual dearth
is what created our casket congregations
that pushes us on the path
of destructions destination

but I can feel original love's
trillionth's gestation
and if you can't guess
it's coming from all locations

Cosmic Calligraphy   Born Free

cuz we're combinations of combinations
stars mixed with semen
it's only when the Yoni and Yogi are uneven
that our embryos began to weaken

that why I went out there seeking
natural medicine to extend our season
I just hope I learned enough
before the legions of demon's poison our new Eden

It's Survival of the Fittest

It's survival of the fittest
gotta learn how to pivot
the witless got skittish
I spit a verse in Yiddish

then I finished my spinach
marinated in garlic
I watch what I think
because life is Karmic

discarded dead weight
toned up got straight
fresh god degree
on grandma's old plates

I opened my floodgates
increased my growth rate
now destiny and fate
are both my soulmates

Black Monolith's

Black monolith's
were born at the moment of creation
YAH whispered in their essence
the secret to perfect communication

he placed them before the beginning
of all our scientific advancements
they sparked all our imagination
and enchantments

these black monoliths
are indefinable
they are transcendent
and indescribable

terrifying to some
intriguing to most
interplanetary signposts
keys to the cosmos

the surface is new and smooth
the color of triple stage darkness
life and death
spring from the catharsis

some were placed in space
some were placed on all landscapes
some were placed right offshore
some were placed deep inside your core

don't be afraid of them
they are a part of life's universal plan
as they approach
your mind will expand

Cosmic Calligraphy   Born Free

respect the architect
be humble, come correct
don't inspect to dissect
you're in the presence of the divinely perfect

YAH imbued them with a jewel
that fuels every human break through
you must be able to look at the familiar shape
as something completely brand new

these black monoliths
are only with us for a quick flash
so either embrace the next phase
or prepare to be buried with the past

Portals of Prayer

I travel through portals of prayer

I sidestep misery's affairs
I'm protected from the devil's
day and nightmares
I can find somewhere out of nowhere
I see the circle inside the square
because when I meditate on God's word
I feel as free and light as air

I travel through portals of prayer

it doesn't matter what I wear
my attitude is nude
and I'm right here
I'm present and open
my soul only desires to share
the power and brilliance of God's universe
cannot be compared

I travel through portals of prayer

all my sins have been laid bare
my truth has been declared
my broken heart is being repaired
devil beware
I have come for the ensnared
supplication and formations
prepares me for all forms of warfare

My Approach

My approach to writing is clear
I'm never cautious
some applaud this
others get nauseous

I never try to force this
I know where my source is
the rabbit mind is blind
put your money on the tortoise

we might move a little slower
but we're the most consistent
infant missions
will get you blown out of position

beloved listen
move efficient
cuz the ground and life beneath
your feet are shiftin

we're coexisting
with all beings and lifeforms
and that's why I spread love
on every platform

so, when I see white supremacy
I swarm
cuz won't let another young mind and heart
be niggerized and deformed

so, beloved listen
move efficient
cuz the ground and life beneath
your feet are shiftin

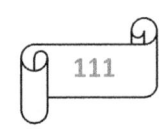

Journal Entry #14

I logged off the server
fortified my girders
got back to the basics
manners prevent murder

the Judaic herder
taking the tribe further
teach with books and burners
YAH's divine worker

Head to the Stars

Head to the stars
reading God's memoirs
flying with the avatars
droppin seeds in bars

it's been a minute
since Washington's new tenant
hate's epidemic
modern eugenics

schizophrenic chemists
poisoned traps in academics
I have no limits
and I'll never be finished

the essence of Godly physics
manifested in my image
you can praise my hieroglyphics
but God is the most prolific

My Cosmic Calligraphy

My cosmic calligraphy
helps me see life's symmetry
but I don't use those epiphanies
to escape harsh realities

my panoramic agility
universal ministry
is to defeat self-hate's malignancy
and vanquish white supremacy

some use otherworldly imagery
to slide into invisibility
so they don't have to deal
with poverty and brutality

it's a cowardly
form of toxicity
to cosmically
ignore earthly calamities

it's a tragedy
to only track the heavenly anatomy
when you won't sit down
and create sustainable life strategies

why spend your time
with Tarot technologies
when you won't use it to figure out
how to feed hungry families

Cosmic Calligraphy   Born Free

please don't let your knowledge of alchemy
become impotent spiritual vanity
because no one what's to hear about the galaxy
if we can't use it to break free of earthly captivity

so, my cosmic calligraphy
is not about sci-fi fantasy
it's about how I can tangibly and drastically
change the lives of my community

Without Love, Faith, and Action

Without love, faith, and action
your knowledge becomes an irrelevant maze
a library of dead theories
suffocated by an incomprehensible haze
acquiring knowledge to only debate
gives you no value, connection, or protection
it's love, faith, and action
that gives your knowledge purpose, power, and direction

Capricorn One

What happens after
we determine it was fake
do we just want to know
for knowledge's sake

or do we say
I told you so
spit another righteous flow
and write another manifesto

upload another YouTube video
with a link to another Vimeo
hold court at the Barbershop
about the new Jim and Jane Crow

beloved, our thoughts have plateaued
confused substance with shadows
we've become super smart
no show's

it's time to grow
build a building while we're building
the soil doesn't need defining
it needs tilling

our position in 2022
is chilling
no wonder why we can't
stop the killing

Cosmic Calligraphy　　　　　　Born Free

them killing us
and us killing us
it's time to adjust
everything has already been discussed

so, what happens after
we determine Capricorn One was all lies
are we just content with being
the original and most wise

what happens after
we reveal the evil grand schemes
are we satisfied
with just creating another viral meme

what happens after
Fauci and Biden are exposed
are we cool
with just saying the emperor has no clothes

what happens after
we reveal the conspiracy to end all conspiracies
are we happy
with just knowing the truth while living on our knees

what happens after
what happens after
what happens after
what happens after…

Journal Entry #15

If you want to open your universal locks
and give birth to your own universal locksmiths
you must develop, safeguard, and nourish
your own creation story, legends, and myths

I See Revelation in this Conversation

I see revelation
in this conversation
and if you have a little patience
I'll tell you my motivations

my foundation is God
that charts my course
infinite energy flows
from that source

my pen is always charged
vision enlarged
But Time Will Reveal
#DeBarge!

I'm forging a fluorescent testament
lyrical antidepressants
fresh PRO-SEEDS
for future investments

land to expand
become God's herald
my next level is to get nestled
where the Israelites settled

so don't back petal
cut the strings of Geppetto
my goal is to grow
without becoming the next devil

Shards of Glass

Even in this shattered state
I still contain the essence of what I am
even the smallest bits of me can still remember
the covenant between God and Abraham
when I was mercilessly thrown to the floor
they thought I would be no more
they believed that the destruction of my body
would give them victory in this spiritual war

they were fuckin wrong!

the silver lining in getting hurt
bruised and fractured before
is that I know that the wretched hands of evil
cannot reach or touch my core
and with my spirit intact
I can summon home all my severed parts
I send out messages to the supreme mind
and she injects the medicine directly in my heart

slowly but surely
I can feel myself reassembling
pieces of my crystal body might be trembling
but that won't stop my reckoning
and just like Jacob wrestling
a new me is developing
for the devils that hurt me it's unsettling
but for the God within me, it's welcoming

Cosmic Calligraphy   Born Free

I thought that being shards of glass
would finish me at last
but I am stronger
because I survived my tragic past
I am not impervious to pain
and I don't deny that I still cry sometimes
but no matter what happens today or tomorrow
I know that I will be fine

Organic Therapeutics

I spark organic therapeutics
through poetry and music
I clear out your mucus
with a spirit/flesh infusion
being human is all consumin
but it's a part of the grand illusion
it's only when the soul is bloomin
that this life is truly movin

and when I say grand illusion
I don't mean that everything is fake
I'm saying that going beneath the surface
is how you become and stay awake
the inner earthquake that occurs
is for both him and hers
if you want to get rid of that blur
allow God to be your chauffeur

Interstellar Siddurs

I read from interstellar Siddurs
the original Shema Yisrael
this is where Almighty God first wrote
how all the prophesies would be fulfilled

Adonai seeded the stars
with the first creation stories
every morning you can bear witness
to the resurrection in all its glory

every light beam
is the magnificence of Elohim
all the glory of life goes to God
for he is supreme

when I read the Heavenly skies
my prayers grow wings and fly
inside our mythologies is a truth
that will never die

Adonai is the beginning and ending
and everything in-between
my prayers reveal to me
that life is and isn't a dream

Adonai is the beginning and ending
and everything in-between
my prayers reveal to me
that life is and isn't a dream

NINA

I've downloaded Nina Simone
right into my bones
so whenever I write poems
you can hear her moan
you can feel her commitment
you can feel her pigment
you can feel her Lamentations
you can feel her destroying false expectations
you can feel her Mississippi Goddamn
you can feel her plan to kill Uncle Sam
you can feel her loading up the ammo
you can feel her giving America a death blow
you can feel her deep love for us
you can feel her eminent genius
you can feel her surviving unspeakable abuse
but most of all you can feel her
unbreakable black truth

While We

While we try to discover if the universe
is a hologram or not
we need to discover
why another human being got shot

while we measure the next mountain
its length and height
we need to find out why we let
another human being die of hunger last night

while we argue about String Theory
and put Greene verses Einstein
we need to find out why we can't agree
about climate change in our lifetime

while we ask if there's a multiverse
or if black holes are cosmic doors
we need to truly ask ourselves
why we can't stop waging wars

Ticking Time Bombs

We're ticking time bombs
cuz we didn't listen to Major Tom
we killed ourselves over petty qualms
cuz we couldn't live our Psalms

we could preach them
and teach them
but we couldn't
live them

which is the point
and purpose
faith without works
is a bloody and murderous circus

we've done our children a disservice
we purchased this new Auschwitz furnace
cuz we happily followed
our favorite pretty and earnest serpents

and we knew they were serpents
they didn't have to fool us
we wanted what we wanted
so we lied to us

we lied to ourselves
and tried to blame them for this hell
but in all reality
we are the reason humanity fell

Toda Raba

Toda Raba
word to the Father
it seems like the devil
hired his own squad of Brahma's

his own squad of leaders
his own squad of preachers
his own squad of healers
his own squad of teachers

and he has his own chessboard
and he knows how to play
we need to get up to God
and speed today

we've been castaways
for far too long
please remember that Wise Intelligent
makes more than just rap songs

Toda Raba
word to the Father
it seems like the children of God
won't stop worshipping the dollar

we won't stop lusting over it
we won't stop putting everything under it
we won't stop lying and cheating to get it
we won't stop killing life to keep it

Cosmic Calligraphy   Born Free

and the more blood money
that gets washed and digitized
the more life
gets discarded and marginalized

and we've been on this monstrous path
for far too long
we need to remember that
Psalms are more than just church hymns and songs

It's More Than One

It's more than one Wheel

cuz it's more than one vision
it's more than one Malcolm
cuz they built more than one prison
it's more than one chance
cuz we make more than one mistake
it's more than one choice
cuz we have more than one fate
it's more than one garden
cuz we planted more than one seed
it's more than one crop
cuz it's more than one mouth to feed
it's more than one sign
cuz it's more than one road
it's more than one prayer
cuz the devil stole more than one soul

Journal Entry #16

I know it's hard to talk to your loved ones
about the issues that plague your heart
but it must be done
before what God brought together
we let foolishly fall apart

Love Level Vibrational Venting

A lot of my family and friends
really dislike my pen
if it was up to them
I would never write another quote again

I would never write another poem again
I would never write another verse again
I would never put out another book again
they act like they want it all to end

and I've never been directly dismissed
they just act like my work doesn't exist
which makes me feel
a little sad and pissed

and I don't think they're jealous
mean spirited or spiteful
they just don't give a fuck
about the same dreams that I do

I'm not saying they don't love me
I know for a fact that they do
they just don't see me
the way I do

I'm not their favorite writer
I'm not on their creative radar
they silently wish me well
from afar

Cosmic Calligraphy   Born Free

I try not to think about it
I try to focus on new worlds to discover
but right when my heart starts to recover
they send me a quote from some other mother fucka

they send me a link
to check out some other mother fucka
I be like,
are you serious mother fucka

then they say, Born I thought about you
when I read these incredible lines
I just say thank you
and wonder if I'm losing my fuckin mind

I wonder if I'm wasting my fuckin time
why am I at the back of my friend's line
why do they feel everybody else's work
but not mine

I wish I had the answer
this love level vibrational venting is going on too long
I should just go back
to going along to get a long

because why do I even care
why do I keep trying to share
God gave me this gift
God gave me this chair

I will not die from dejection
I will not let my closest friends bring me down
I will not let my closest friend's silence
slow me down

my chin will stay up
my eyes focused on God's domain
and the supreme glory of his reign
heals all my personal pain

and I know they love me
and I know we're lifelong friends
but I wish that nine books in four years
was important to them

Yes, that's right!

nine books in four years
All Praises Due to the Lord
you can accomplish a lot
when you're being ignored!

P.S.

it's no love lost
no names will ever be revealed
but if this shit hits you different
maybe we should sit down and build

Lost in the Space Between Our Ears

Lost in the space between our ears
lost in the space between our fears
lost in the space between our triangles and squares
lost in the space between our prayers

4.54 billion years into existence
and we still have a stupid love resistance
poor human transmissions
and vicious murder statistics

we're into some sick shit
we're the only species to pollute the water
we need to survive
we're the only species to pollute the air
we need to survive
we're the only species to pollute the food
we need to survive
we're the only species to pollute the land
we need to survive

humans are into some sick shit

we act like we're not from here
we act like we hate this blue sphere
but we do love fashionable war gear
and seductive satanic puppeteers

why are we so scared to openly care for each other
why do we prefer to be shallow lovers
why do we physically and digitally attack each other
when truth is waiting to be discovered

we rather use emoji emotions
emoticon automatons
drinking Arnim Zola Coca Cola
masturbating on the sofa
sucking on virtual areola's
eating Soylent Green Granola
sprinkling Covid and Ebola
on our bread with Mazola

we haven't moved an iota
with all the time God has given us
so far humanity as a whole
has been a bust

and I know it's always exceptions
it's always anomalies
but exceptions and anomalies
don't write constitutions and policies
they don't write and enforce laws
the unevolved do
they don't manage our money
the unevolved do
they don't run our healthcare
the unevolved do
they don't govern the globe
the unevolved do
they don't run the military
the unevolved do
they don't fund our children's education
the unevolved do
they don't control the media
the unevolved do
they don't control natural resources
the unevolved do

Cosmic Calligraphy   Born Free

and that's why I say without hesitation
that we're,

lost in the space between our ears
lost in the space between our fears
lost in the space between our triangles and squares
lost in the space between our prayers

4.54 billion years into existence
and we still have a stupid love resistance
poor human transmissions
and vicious murder statistics

Journal Entry #17

I have no definite answers
just a greater desire to ask questions
so far love, pain, birth, and loss have taught me
the most profound lessons

I Don't Have any Icy Bezels

I don't have any icy bezels
I have celestial rose petals
lavender crystals
that ward off all devils

I count amongst the pebbles
where we remember the fundamentals
we're the greatest teachers
with millions of cracks in our vessel

the metal that created my blade
was fashioned before the crusades
before the slave trade
before King and Chief got played

and I don't care if you're paid
or your brand of topical shade
I refuse to let you assholes
destroy what God made

I Write Doctrines

I write doctrines
high off bee pollen
strong enough
to rebuild the gods on Patmos Island
Judah, The Lion
in Arkham Asylum
teaching the silenced
the true science of self-reliance

The Streets Don't Care about Black People

The streets don't care
about black people
they turn the righteous and regal
into slaves in Satan's cathedrals

the streets are lethal
created to mislead you
destroy you, kill you
plant the seeds of death within you

this can't continue
lowered standards are disasters
the new black movement
is black lives shattered

black blood splattered
black bodies battered
black body bags
filled with young black cadavers

black souls captured
black prayers unanswered
because we traded the black God
for the white god enamored

they reprogramed Hip-Hop's grammar
the rappers cooperated
they get compensated
for pushin the fatally fabricated

they get elevated
the more black lives are terminated
this can't be overstated
it's all orchestrated

Cosmic Calligraphy   Born Free

the audience participates
acting out hate's mandates
turning more God's to niggas
creating a new race of rich primates

a new nation of inmates
skyrocketing murder rates
killing off our own future greats
is how the system operates

I pray this translates
don't believe in the deceitful
cuz the streets don't care
about black people

what we're doing to each other
is unspeakable
and the streets don't care
about black people

don't fill your bassinets
with Opioids and drug needles
cuz the streets don't care
about black people

we can't continue to let Hip-Hop
be white supremacy's vehicle
cuz the streets don't care
about black people

the devil is powerful
but he's beatable
and the streets don't care
about black people

protecting black drug dealers
over black babies is evil
and the streets don't care
about black people

making gang culture pop culture
is also evil
and the streets don't care
about black people

love and the word of God
has become illegal
cuz the streets don't care
about black people

the streets don't care
about black people
the streets don't care
about black people
the streets don't care
about black people
the streets don't care
about black people
the streets don't care
about black people
the streets don't care
about black people
the streets don't care
about black people
the streets don't care
about black people

Don't Run from Yourself

Don't run from yourself
you contain more than you can fathom
climb down inside your darkest cavern
swim inside every bright atom

everything isn't for mass consumption
every thought isn't up for discussion
but everything is a part of your total construction
everything inside you has a function

nobody is perfect
I'll say that again
nobody is perfect
but we're all worth it
our true value comes from
God beneath the surface

don't be so hard on yourself
be honest and own your actions
after that you can't be responsible
for the next person's reaction

don't run from yourself
don't accept this worlds reduction
push through their obstructions
fuck their presumptions

everything that you go through is an instruction
letting people distract you is self-destruction
what you know about yourself thus far
has just been an introduction

What Scares me the Most

What scares me the most
isn't the vaccination
it's that we must blindly accept
governmental proclamations

we must accept their explanations
because we don't have independent means
we must take at face value
what comes from this 400-year racist machine

what comes from our phones and TV screens
what comes down these digital streams
I can't believe that we still must buy
these GMO un-magical beans

it makes me want to scream
in the middle of my morning call on Teams
because our movement towards independence
is fading away like a dream

even if you get the shot
and you openly say you have more questions
an avalanche of hate
comes down hard in your direction

and I'm NOT anti-vax
I'm PRO counterattack
we must independently verify
so-called verified facts

but what really scares me the most
is that we're producing more and more mental slaves
and the smart idiots among us
are hating and debating each other into the grave

Everyone Knows

Everyone knows that faith
without works is worthless and stillborn
but we keep harvesting
all that poisonous corn

everyone knows that the devil
is a mother fuckin liar
but we keep believing
that he wants a peaceful ceasefire

everyone knows that white supremacy
can't be remixed and reformed
but we keep acting as if individual banking
means group power is transferred and transformed

knowing what's going on is one thing
doing something about it is something else
we need to accept the reality that the devil
will never give the children of God any real help

Connectivity

Yes, we're all connected
physical and electric
billions of different perspectives
but a part of the same human collective

light, particles, atoms
molecules, cells, and skin
no matter where you're from
this is the container we're all in

of course, we come in different
sizes, shapes, and shades
but when it comes to our true essence
it's all a masquerade

analog or digital
wire or wireless
we're failing the test
to connect beneath the flesh

to help feather our neighbor's nest
to do what our lips profess
to see the supreme value in our hearts
we must invest, invest, invest

to suggest that we're just individuals
is cosmically criminal
and one of the key reasons
we struggle to manifest miracles

Cosmic Calligraphy

it is the invisible
that births the visible
and creates the natural balance
that's always reciprocal

this wisdom is not whimsical
it's a kaleidoscope of wonder
that merges the over and under
and removes all false buffers

we're affected by each other
galactic sisters and brothers
I pray that Covid gave you the clarity
that we cannot survive without each other

what you do affects me
what I do affects you
we don't have to agree on everything
to understand this point of view

so yes, we're all connected
physical and electric
billions of different perspectives
but a part of the same human collective

I know you can see it
I know you can feel it in your deepest regions
if we can't connect our lives and teachings
this might be our last and most tragic season

Journal Entry #18

I used to hate all my scars
I thought they were ugly
but now I adore them
because they remind me
that I survived
the most difficult times in my life

We're Greater

We're greater than the Sorcerer Supreme
we're the first born of Almighty Elohim
while we were charting stars and mapping light beams
the Greeks played carelessly in the young Nile streams

before science was called science
and before religion was dogmatized
it was your ways and actions
that determined if you were intelligent and wise

we traveled the galaxy
in Kemetic astral planes
we knew that the Creator
had an unpronounceable name

so, we used our souls to speak
and YHWH responded through our hearts and mind
and said that if we love self and our neighbors
love, peace, and happiness will never be hard to find

Ultra-Magnetic

I'm ultra-magnetic
it was formed in my genetics
whenever you hear the truth
you know that YHWH said it
my aesthetic is poetic
unapologetic, epic
I write the prophetic
you suck the synthetic
kinetic cosmic consciousness
third eye oculus
fuck the devil
I'm on top of this
my confidence
is bottomless
I said, FUCK the devil
I'm on top of this

I Dip My Pen in Blood

I dip my pen in blood
because I speak from my heart
channel God, love and hurt
because that's where I start

it's amazing how pain
never truly goes away
even though you're light years
from that tragic day

and it's been hard for me
not to let bitterness build a home inside
and slowly magnify
my ego, hurt feelings, and false pride

it's a daily grind
to move forward and not keep looking behind
but it's a must if I want to have
peace of spirit, peace of heart, and peace of mind

With Each Inscription

With each inscription
I overwrite the fiction
that demonized my description
and caused all crucifixions
our latest addiction
was authorized in every jurisdiction
and that's why I had to drop
a brand-new glorious edition

Flat or Round?

The earth is flat
no, the earth is round
but what does it matter
when these young kids are being buried in the ground

the earth is flat
no, the earth is round
but what does it matter
when the lost have never been found

we say we enter these debates
based on knowledge, science, and faith
but they quickly become the face
of anger, ignorance, and hate

and while we're arguing tooth and nail
more young toes are tagged
hearts are broken
young bodies are bagged

whether it's flat or round
how much of it is ours
the blame can't be placed at the feet of the stars
for giving our kids those deadly scars

endless seminars
won't supply our demands
they won't assure our victory
or place us in command

Cosmic Calligraphy   Born Free

these discussions be damned
when dealing with murdered lives
we can't use knowledge to hide
cuz we're afraid of the devil outside and inside

now I can't lie
I love a great build
this book is a testament
to old and future prophecies revealed

but when you're on the battlefield
and blood is being spilled
you must have a spiritual
and a physical shield

food for thought
can't be our only meal
I mean more than a metaphor
when I say, steel sharpens steel

but they still want to argue
that the earth is flat
in the face of our children
being held back

they still want to argue
that the earth is round
when we are killing ourselves
in every fuckin town

it's one of the dumbest
debates on the market
because how does this knowledge
stop our children from being a target

Cosmic Calligraphy   Born Free

so yeah, the earth is flat
no, the earth is round
but what does it matter
when these young kids are being buried in the ground

the earth is flat
no, the earth is round
but what does it matter
when the lost have never been found

Journal Entry #19

Rigid theories
are more damaging than unsubstantiated ones
without the possibility of being wrong
new revelations will never come

Stargates

Stargates aren't something
buried in the African sands
they are pathways
submerged in the murky waters of man

no need to scan the symbols and glyphs
that's not how you receive the portals gifts
you must manifest the qualities of God
to qualify to go on these internal celestial trips

The Root Chakra (Muladhara) – Red Color/396 Hz

The root chakra
is your foundational chakra
it's where you begin your quest
to re-merge with YAH
when you mediate at this point
you increase your security and stability
to open the next six
you must make your root chakra a priority
it helps shed all the shame and regret
fear and guilt
it will help you clear the way
for your life to be re-built
when your roots are healthy
your tree of life will flourish
so as you begin this wonderful adventure
make sure your root connection to earth is nourished

Sacral Chakra (Svadhishthana) – Orange Color/417 Hz

When your sensuality is blooming
and you're comfortable feeling and expressing pleasure
your sacral chakra has flowered
and you can delight in your body's treasures
you can feel it in your lower abdomen
your bladder, kidneys, and genitals
it's the physical manifestation
of the sensual and spiritual
when your sacral chakra
is undeveloped and impeded
you might try to overcompensate
and become even more depleted
but when it's balanced
and properly ignited
the needs of your spirit and body
are at peace and united

Solar Plexus Chakra (Manipura) –Yellow Color/528 Hz

This is your power center
your control center
but it's some things about your power
you must always remember
the power that emanates from this chakra
isn't about domination and manipulation
it's about your ability to be confident
and the firmness of your determination
when your solar plexus
is in alignment
you'll break free
from all the chains of confinement
and this power is not to be used
to bully or demean
your solar energy is there to fuel
your highest expression of self-belief and self-esteem

The Heart Chakra (Anahata) – Green Color/639 Hz

The journey through the heart
is a journey through infinite joy and compassion
self-acceptance, universal acceptance
and spiritual expansion
when your heart chakra is open
and functioning at its highest degree
you will feel an immense flow
of warm spiritual energy
your healthy relationships will grow
your unhealthy relationships will dissipate
you will feel lighter
because you dropped those bags of dead weight
and when your emotions find equilibrium
you will be able to handle resistance
these are all the signs
that your heart chakra is open for business

The Throat Chakra (Vishuddha) – Blue Color/741 Hz

When your throat chakra is open
your communication will astound
even the simplest phrases
will be profound
your voice will be strong
your thyroid will find balance
and the things that you want to say
won't be a challenge
whether it's verbal or non-verbal
external or internal
when you speak and express
the understanding will be universal
Almighty God is always sending you messages
that need to be translated
so keep your throat chakra open
so his truth can be communicated

The Third Eye Chakra (Ajna) – Indigo Color/852 Hz

The third eye is lidless
it doesn't get tired or distracted
your third eye can guide you
when your other eyes are enchanted
when you meditate at this level
your empathy and intuition expand
you will listen and not just hear
you will think to understand
the black dot
is in the center of your forehead
it sees beyond the words
and connects to the intention behind what is said
your awareness will sharpen
you will move beyond mystical jargon
you will see and experience abundance
grow beautifully in your spiritual garden

The Crown Chakra (Sahasrara) – Violet Color/963 HZ

When you experience the violet vibration
abound in the realm of the crown
you will finally realize
how we can turn everything around
you dissolve into your original state
a blank slate
just infinite possibilities
a virgin field to cultivate
can't you feel the magnitude
of everything and NO-THINGS
existing without form
no body, no brain, and no wings
in Kabbalah we call this place, The Ein-Sof
but it goes by thousands of names
the crown chakra leads to the holy of holies
it is what sustains all life's eternal flame

Prayers and Meditation Work

Prayers and meditation work
your spiritual energy is boundless
when we pray and meditate together
the force of God's love surrounds us
the skies become cloudless
we get a glimpse of life's true essence
when we pray and meditate together
we disappear and reappear in God's Holy presence

Who or What Guides You

Who or what guides you
who or what motivates your movements
who or what can confidently call you
their student
who or what do you listen too
who or what gave you a staff
who or what do you submit too
and put you on your current path

Sacred Timeline

White Supremacy
bombed the Sacred Timeline
nexus level events
altered our original minds

variants of ourselves
exploded across the Multiverse
some versions were revolutionary
some versions were perverse

some were brilliant
some were six short of a dozen
all versions became everything that was
and wasn't

some were divine workers
some were everyday observers
some were universal searchers
some were bloody murderers

white supremacy nurtured
our most self-destructive versions
and killed off any of us
who fought for our unified resurgence

white supremacy cultivated
each of these broken branches
to secure more war
and advance interplanetary expansion

at first we were first
then enslavement grafted us to be the worse

changing the timeline changed the paradigms
and we felt like we were naturally cursed

the tragic inhuman trafficking
savage inhuman repackaging
in Africa and the diaspora
God's original cultures started vanishing

from whole people
to fragments
human fractions
can never gain collective traction

but we must take action
intergalactic and local
cuz they are the global Chernobyl's
moguls of the woeful

my proposal
is to prune them on sight
reset the sacred timeline
and bring balance to the left and right

this is a lifelong fight
some variants have joined their side
it's sad but inevitable
that some of us variants will collide

some of us variants will die
quite frankly I'm terrified
but whether we multiply or nullify
the timeline must be rectified

too much time has passed by
but we can't comply
look to God and not the Timekeepers
as your ally

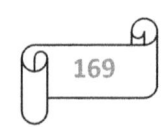

Cosmic Calligraphy　　　　　　　　　Born Free

reject the T.V.A
they move like S.W.A.T.
they are a part of the trap
white supremacy's sub-plot

we will untie our own knots
we will deal with our own variants
lock arms around us
the gregarious and nefarious

the Annunaki's to the Loki's
high strung and low key's
Ice Cube's and Smokey's
Fannie Lou's and Cokely's

we run the gambit
of human expression
re-crashing the timeline
will change our current direction

but we can never go back
to exactly the way it was before
everything has changed
including the door

but realigning our timeline
puts us on a different path
for better or worse
we must get on a different path

but we can't go back to the past
we can't get everything back that was stolen
but we can create a new life
some new golden moments

so if you're ready, I'm ready
set as many charges as you can
God will always be with us
cuz ultimately this is all a part of his plan

LET ME SAY THAT AGAIN!

if you're ready, I'm ready
set as many charges as you can
God will always be with us
cuz ultimately this is all a part of his plan

Sage and Soldiers

You better have sage and soldiers
bill folders and gun toters
cuz as I get older
I see that victory is in the eye of the beholder
get voters and digital coders
Yoda's and flame throwers
but without black social theory composers
we'll be murdered with machine guns and modems

I Fly Like a Falcon

I fly like a falcon
move like a stallion
Deuteronomy 6:4
engraved on my medallion
march in God's battalion
our swords are drawn
clips fully loaded
wicked blood floods the lawn
this is not for the squeamish
or the sheepish
those who choose gold over God
are the weakest
the deepest jewels
are always the most basic lessons
like don't count your problems
count your blessin's
always be grateful
not hateful
always say a prayer
over the food on your table
this is how we'll make it
this is how I flow
faith, friendship, forgiveness
are some of the best fruits I grow

What If...

Marvel asked What If...
let me tell you how it is
our decisions can either free
or imprison our kids
and until my eyelids close
I'll work to expose Adonai's foes
cuz I made an oath to God in the cave
where The Black Christ first rose

Journal Entry #20

We're all flammable
but we all have the power to burn
we're all fallible
but we all have the capacity to learn

no matter where you are
on the line of morality
we all contain a mustard seed
of divine spirituality

Liquid Science

From liquid Swords
to liquid science
I write to give guidance
older than the first children of Zion
I was living the Torah
before the Nephilim's were called giants
my Abrahamic alliance
will give you triumph over tyrants
in silence and darkness
is where my power was harnessed
the skies were starless
the process was cathartic
my old skin was shed
a cocoon surrounded my new form
disconnecting from the Covenant
is the only way I'll miss the upcoming dawn

Sisters of the Valley

Sisters of the Valley
nuns who grow weed
we met up at the rally
they always give me what I need
we pray first
then spark the herbal essence
exorcising the accursed
is the anti-depressant
CBD oil
safe, non-addictive
peace is in the soil
the cure for man's sickness
I love these women
God gave them a divine mission
the perfect blend
removes all opposition

Sisters of the Valley
nuns of the fellowship
sun, moon, and earth
natural science is rich
Beguines Queens
cultivating clean vaccines
pushin love and life
by any means
dreams of Cannabis commerce
brings hope to the dearth
investing in the youth
increasing self-love and self-worth
a rebirth of the spirit
the rebuilding of the mind
when you righteously sow with nature
you reap the harvest of the divine

Sisters of the Valley
nuns with life nurseries
they're winning
because of God's mercy
they protected the crops with prayers
they protected the crops with sage
they protected the crops with lawyers
they protected the crops with the gauge
they're engaged
ushering in a new age
where man and earth
write together on the new page
the truth is out the cage
Mother Nature is our liberation
and the enemies of her
are the enemies of God's Holy nation

Sisters of the Valley
nuns with integrity
the bounty from Gaia
is a part of their weaponry
the remedy for suffering
is in the ground beneath your feet
you can medicate grief with a leaf
no more chemicals to sleep
Mary don't you weep
the sisters shepherd good sheep
apply the Salve
before your depression gets deep
chronic pain, anxiety
seizures, PTSD
these beautiful sisters of the valley
are healing the heart of our society

Y'all Can't See Me

Y'all can't see me
I write poetry in graffiti
my pen channels the spirit
of Runoko Rashidi
your Ahki Born Free
Intelligent back bone
I helped move a movement
over the mother fuckin phone
when they heard my voice
they moved the chess pieces
my thesis is Jesus
Queens feed it to their fetus
some call me general Grievous
God made me his phoenix
I move the masses
Hebrew telekinesis

I Can't Turn This Off

I can't turn this off
and wouldn't if I could
don't hate me for pointing out
the termites in the wood
I know I've changed
from the first time we met
you're having second thoughts
your heart is filled with regret
but it cuts me to the quick
to see you take the stand against me
lying to the world
you set fire to our tapestry
but the real tragedy
is when lies and deception is embraced
you cut out your tongue
to despite your taste

On My Glorious Path Back to God

I've given up

trying to figure out why
I'm murdered daily
in another human's eyes

for if I have done you wrong
lay your testimony at my feet
show me where I have not
shared my milk and meat

show me where I have tried
to sabotage your victories
show me where I have betrayed
our bonded history

because if you can't
unhitch yourself from my side
spread your wings
mother fucka, fly

because I won't live and die
wondering why you don't like me
why you don't love me
or why you don't want me

get the fuck away from me
I don't tolerate facades
cuz you're just a small pebble
on my glorious path back to God

Each One of my Books

Each one of my books
contain my blood and flesh
communion on Easter
my thoughts are dressed to impress

but not for the ego
touchin the souls of the people
cuz these GMO Neo's
feed us placebo's

they use God's lingo
to distract and disarm
they would sell you Air Force One
before they sell you a farm

the devil's charms
silence your alarms
only time will tell
what we injected in our arms

they spin the stickiest yarns
tell believable lies
make you idolize the uncivilized
and scandalize God's prize

my work is for the butterflies
and the caterpillars
killers, guerrillas
and the distillers in African villages

Cosmic Calligraphy   Born Free

I've been diligent
against the villainous
Deuteronomy 6:4
makes me limitless

Deuteronomy 6:5
makes me the richest
Deuteronomy 10:16
cured my sickness

Deuteronomy 18:9
helps guide my choices
Deuteronomy 4:6
speaks for the voiceless

the pearl in my oyster
handcrafted by the creator
he made me great
cuz he's absolutely GREATOR!!!

I Am the Trend

I am the trend
I depend on God only
I write and rarely speak
cuz I'm watching the phony closely
they mostly talk shit
caught up in stupid endeavors
you can't be a black boss
if you're a black billionaire beggar
I know this verse is a stressor
and hits some points of pressure
but if our leaders aren't leading us to power
they ain't worth the measure
following them is an error
the great debaters must come to a quick end
proper planning and progress
should be the new trend
if we're not moving to
controlling our own demand and supply
we're setting our children up
to be locked up to die
we're setting our children up
to be the footstools of the world
the global mammies
for every other little boy and girl
we're setting our children up
to be the permanent underclass
it doesn't matter who is the original man
when you let your seeds become dead last

Burning the High Table

Burning the High Table
is exquisite sanity
the twelve families at that hellish table
are a vile scourge on humanity

syndicates of corruption
traffickers of guns, guts, and gore
transnational Baphomet's
hideous mid-wives of war

death to the Adjudicators
for the table we're just sport and play
they determine who eats what
and on which days

they make all the rules
they can change all the rules
they sit above the rules
fuck them and their rules

the Walton's, Koch brothers
Mars, D'Antonios
follow the blood money
and the horrible truth will be exposed

they use our bodies in their mills
our spirits power their systems
set us in bloody competition
the victor and victims are both enslaved victims

Cosmic Calligraphy											Born Free

movies, reality
it's all reality
look around you
see and smell the casualties

you know I'm speaking the truth
don't try to cover their crimes
anybody that does
I'm leaving behind

the High Table
must be brought down
all the power and prestige
bury them with melted crowns

FUCK the High Table
I resist and rebuke them all
I can't wait to set it ablaze
and watch God smile when they fall

Parabellum, Parabellum
the power is back in The Bowery King's hands
bury the table, their Presidents, and Elder's
under the hot Moroccan sands

Hard Trials

I'm facing a set of hard trials
but I won't turn away from God
I'm seeing more frowns than smiles
but I won't turn away from God
I've talked a good talk
but that's just the surface part
God knows I love him in the light
but the test is praising him in the dark

One Second

One second you're here
one second you're not
be extremely thankful
for each second you got
life is a revolving door
it's constantly turning and turning
so please make sure
that you're constantly appreciating and learning

Never Lied in my Verses

Never lied in my verses
never misled in my searches
cuz if I did
YAH would hit me with Pharaoh curses

so, calm down your urges
to see me fail, go off the rails
I'm still going to make it to Heaven
with these holes in my sails

I will prevail
won't see any parts of hell
cast off my shell
bid you bloodsucker's farewell

I gave you too much
I gave you my heart unprotected
I should have suspected
that you would leave me infected

disconnected from myself
disturbed my mental health
ya'll turned into Casper's
when I needed some help

but I blame myself
should have trusted God's plan
got needy and greedy
I should have trusted God's plan

Cosmic Calligraphy   Born Free

foolish and coolish
I should have trusted God's plan
naïve and self-deceived
I should have trusted God's plan

but now I see
I'm investing in me
surging and merging
with the entire galaxy

beyond the Silver Surfer
and Galactus
I don't have time
for these fake bastards

love is still my practice
no matter how I've been treated
don't wonder where I've been
you've been deleted

I needed to do that
evolve my whole format
forward forever
I'm not going back

if you want to be with me
come to God first
once you do that
we can break the curse

and if I want you
I must seek God first
and once I do
we can break the curse

Broadcasting

I was never afraid of the age of Ultron
I'm focused on the age of Viacom
and what really happened on 9/11
at the Pentagon

my word is bond
my bond is everlasting
my spirit is broadcasting
when I'm prayin and fastin

I'm surpassin
all those beggin and askin
I'm unmaskin the grafted
while his world is collapsing

it's happenin beloved
I've rediscovered
the first Torah scroll
that Jacob ever uttered

51 Years In

I wish I could see your face
after I physically die
who's going to celebrate
and who's going to cry

who's going to lie
and who's going to confront the liars
who's going to pick up the mantle
and do what God requires

whose love is going to quickly expire
who's going to lift my name higher
who's going to stay true
who's my true riders

I don't know how much time
I have left
I gotta stop arguing with assholes
gotta conserve my breath

51 years in
and I'm still a little guarded
I think it's past time
that I block the cold hearted

even those who I've known
for more years than I can count
must go if they
live inside fear and doubt

this is not judgement
it's the essential selfishness of survival
I don't have any time
for secret wars and quiet rivals

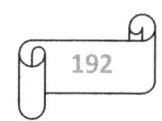

I'm here to shine the light
that God gave me at birth
I can't let anyone
diminish my self-worth

I gotta unearth
my diamonds and gold
I gotta give you
my honest soul

because I don't know
how much time I have left
I can't be afraid
of the truth expressed

because I'm 51 years in
I don't know when or if I'll be back again
I'm 51 years in
I don't know when or if I'll be back again

Be Open

Be open
but be discriminating
be humble
but don't be self-depreciating
be a friend
but don't be an enemy to yourself
be giving
but don't shortchange your own spiritual wealth

Journal Entry #21

My heart's testimony
isn't for those with weak constitutions
you won't understand it
if you're still lost in adolescent illusions

Some Days

I love to go slow
and whisper Heaven in your ears real soft
but some days my love
I need to rip all your clothes off
I need you to feel the intense heat and weight
of my uncontrollable fury
baby, don't take your eyes off me
we're about to redefine ecstasy

fuck a fantasy
this is our reality
you should have known how it would be
when you got with a man named **Born Free**
I AM the galaxy
let me spread your lips with my thumbs
the easiest thing you're going to do tonight
is cum

Love Beckons Us

Love openly beckons us
love set interdimensional traps for us
love wants and needs to be experienced
love hates when it's only discussed

I see love in all things
no matter if it's night or day
I feel love more intensely
when Mercury is in retrograde

when things are out of sync
and flowing against the grain
I tend to call out for more love
in all its languages and names

love lives in all the sky houses
loves speaks in every living tongue
if love corners you on the road of life
consider yourself one of the luckiest ones

You Found Me

Many thought I made a deal with the devil
to get a Queen on your level
unamused and confused
how I found a treasure so special
I told them I put God first
followed the law and not my thirst
and once I did that
you found me and pull me out of the hearse

Journal Entry #22

No one runs into their love randomly
their deep connection makes meetings a certainty
those on the outside call it a one and a million chance
but love knows it's a part of its eternal dance

New Ink...New Design

(Our Old Life)

Before we set fire to our old lives
our old forest
our old homes
our old dreams
our old misconceptions
our old misdirection's
our old miscommunications
our old childish ways
our old regrets
and our old books
let's read one more ancient passage
one more aborted line
one more contradictory word
and remember what could have been
what we could have accomplished
what we could have gained
what we could have seen, tasted, and experienced
and all that wasn't
and then we can finally
grow up and accept
what really went down
and just be done with it
let it all go
let it all burn
let it all return

(Our New Life)

As our old fires starts to dim and die
our new blaze burns brighter than ever before
our new lives begin to flourish
we get stronger and stronger
our new covenant
has the strength and conviction of Abraham
our new hearts have given birth
to a new and higher standard
a new faith
a new and beautiful child of our God
this new creation
is the prototype
for the new evolution of this crude human species
its divine speech vibrates at a pitch
that only true lovers can discern
as our new fire continues to burn
the embers light up the dark sky
and reveal brand new constellations
new dimensions
new galaxies
new possibilities
I've dreamed for so long
to bear witness to a woman's true nudity
and it's turning me on beyond belief
we've actually found the next level
and discovered that's it's just another plateau
let's keep climbing

Journal Entry #23

I don't want to be rational
I don't want to look at the bigger picture
I don't care if we break the furniture
I don't care if I get injured
I need to be inside of you
I need to fly to heaven with you
I need you to understand
that this is what we're created to do

Love Paraphernalia

The cops kicked down the door
but we were nowhere to be found
Metatron tipped us off
and we immediately left town

we're not bound by any of our
wonderful possessions
we didn't have anything that we couldn't leave
in less than 30 seconds

what they found in our sanctuary
stopped them in their tracks
they found a treasure trove
of love's forbidden artifacts

they saw two Peacock chairs
with one large multi-colored blanket
a chess board with the black pieces
converging on a white Queen's Gambit

they found a library of books and music
and a vintage record player
oil paintings of family members
united in solemn prayer

old photos along the walls
of us laughing and dancing over the years
a mantle lined with Valentine cards
and road trip souvenirs

they ripped up our old love notes
poems, Haiku's, and silly jokes

but what they hated the most
was that they couldn't destroy the memory of our hope

they confiscated all our herbs and teas
cases and cases of the most sublime wine
they poured out all the water
that was fresh and alkaline

they threw out all our fruit
and pulled up all our flowers by the root
infuriated by our matching
clothes, shoes, and boots

they violently destroyed our bed
mocked our sex toys and games
smashed all our sweet perfumes
and set our bedroom aflame

we were branded enemies of the state
kill orders were issued
all the items in our homes
were destroyed and discontinued

we eternally thank God
that they never found us
we eternally thank God
that he never left us

we love our new home
we live beyond their savage radar
beyond the first planets
beyond the first stars

Cosmic Calligraphy   Born Free

we exist inside the bosom of God
where love and laughter are business as usual
and hatred and enmity
is unconstitutional

sometimes I pity those storm troopers
they know not what they do
but enough about them
let me get back to loving you

Journal Entry #24

You dream about love and being loved
all day, every day
but are you preparing yourself to be open
for when you decide to get out of love's way

Plant Based Love

Don't ask me how I know
I just know
our communication is warm
and it just flows

we're from the old and new Eden
we bathe in the Euphrates
this is the kind of love
that keeps your seeds out of Hades

we thick like vegan gravy
low fat, high fiber
two of our sex names
are the wolf and the spider

we shine brighter
rational and irrational
we feed our God
and our animal

our love is natural
organic, essential
the physical is manifested
from the spiritual

the mental
firm but gentle
when our hearts assemble
we build new temples

transcendental
monumental

Cosmic Calligraphy   Born Free

we've made it this far
cuz we're nonjudgmental

the uninitiated tremble
damn near disassemble
they have the bells and whistles
but lack the fundamentals

nothing about us is coincidental
we're providence's prophesy
we transcend IG oddities
our soul's symmetry is sacred geometry

our love's anatomy
has no artificial additives
our spirits are in balance
we reject social media narratives

no pesticides
no plastic packages
our bodies and souls are fortified
against governmental pathogens

our relatives
are of God and Gaia's creation
our love extends the line
of future generations

we are the combination
of all elemental forces
even our disagreements
reinforces what the source is

what the force is
Ein Sof and Nirvana
we're protected
from all the worldly drama

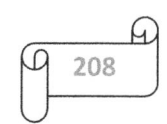

our Karma
conjoined the light and dark
we inherited this love
to protect the universal spark

the hallmark of our blessing
is always expressing
we fly through different worlds
leaving the lost confused and guessing

for most it's depressing
because separation is a curse
they want to knock over our cup
cuz their lungs bitterly thirst

but if they just put God first
they would immediately see
that loving each other is the path
to bringing harmony back to the family

did you hear me?

if they just put God first
they would immediately see
that loving each other is the path
to bringing harmony back to the family

Journal Entry #25

When I finally stood in love's glorious presence
I realized I had been a fool for many-many years
when I finally shed the dead skin of bitterness
I realized I had cut my own throat with my own shears
when I finally shut my swollen mouth
I realized I had been butchering love's righteous name
when I finally stepped back into love's radiant light
I realized I had been cursing out old shadows in vain

Be

B*e Quiet*
Be Still
Be Ready
Be Open

Be Quiet
Be Still
Be Ready
Be Open

Be Quiet
Be Still
Be Ready
Be Open

Be Quiet
Be Still
Be Ready
Be Open

Be Open
Be Open
Be Open
Be Open

The Fountain

Our love has always existed
we were married before the first before
our first mutual orgasm
opened up new worlds to explore
and when your beautiful form started to fade
I found the fountains cure
and when I reached the precipice of old age
you guided me back through the Morrison's door
a love like ours
stops the curse of darkness's decent
a love like ours
brings life and death together in agreement
a love like ours
can't be adjusted or detoured
a love like ours
was sealed by the first kiss of our Lord

we always recognize each other
no matter how much time has passed
time has no hold or quarrel with us
it only destroys what fools try to horde and amass
we've been Kemetic, Ethiopian
Ghanaian, Jamaican
European, Californian
Indian and Philadelphian
we lived with the Eternal's
and fought against King Leopold
stood against the evil of Columbus and Washington
our love was foretold
but most ignored our prophecy
called it a simple allegory
they didn't understand that God sent us
to finish his divine story

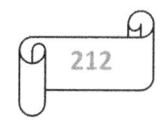

Us Against the World

It's us against the world
we have our own front and back
when you come against me
she goes on the attack

every morning we train
meditate and build
we pray constantly
cuz God is the strongest shield

I'm not talking about blocking bullets
I'm talking about surviving the war on all levels
evil wins in the end
if our PTSD breeds a new crop of young devils

cuz it's us against the world
we have our own front and back
when you come against her
I go right on the attack

Think Beloved, Think! (message to my brothers)

Think beloved, think
your whole life is on the line
I want the same thing for you
that I want for me and mine
in fact, I want you to live
more abundantly than I
think about what you're doing
I don't want you to die

we all make mistakes
we sometimes choose the wrong fate
but if you continue down that way
you'll only find darkness and death in your wake
don't let your anger consume you
don't let this moment become a catastrophe
because throwing away all that you could become
would be the worst kind of tragedy

Heavy

Heavy is the head
that wears earthly crowns
heavy is the body
when it's gunned down
heavy is the heart
when you get those calls
heavy are the tears
when a young god falls

life is too precious
don't play those street games
cuz it takes shorter than you think
for the street to forget your name
even if they salute you
and give you a beautiful mural
they will not take care of your family
after the funeral
they will beef with each other
over whom gets to fuck your wife
corrupt your children
and darken their light
every opportunity in these streets
ends with you paying the ultimate price
America lets you play in the street
because the streets devour black life

and heavy is the head
that wears earthly crowns
heavy is the body
when it's gunned down

heavy is the heart
when you get those calls
heavy are the tears
when a young god falls

my flow is still pyroclastic
because the times are still drastic
and we're giving birth to more children
inside walking dead caskets
we've been mastered
nothing seems to matter
I already told you that the new black movement
is black lives shattered
we've taken God out of the equation
removed his words from the conversation
and you wonder why
black bodies are piling up around the nation
beloved, every opportunity in these streets
ends with all of us paying the ultimate price
America lets you play in the street
because the streets devour black life

and heavy is the head
that wears earthly crowns
heavy is the body
when it's gunned down
heavy is the heart
when you get those calls
heavy are the tears
when a young god falls

All is Not Lost

All is not lost
I know what I just said on the previous page
but nothing can stop us
if we truly want to change
all is not lost
we have the power to begin again
the devil doesn't have the ability
to defeat the God that I believe in
all is not lost
the devil's strength
comes from our silence and submission
take back your power
align yourself with God's vision
cuz all is not lost
darkness will yield to the light
all is not lost
we must endure through this fight

I Will

I will not succumb
I will not run
I will not forgo
I will not go numb
I will not concede
I will not relinquish
I will not abandon
I will not perish
I will not give in
I will not capitulate
I will not cower
I will not forsake
I will not unravel
I will not buckle
I will not fade away
I will not crumble

BUT!

I will grow
I will ascend
I will advance
I will rise again
I will conquer
I will aspire
I will fly with the angels
I will survive the fire
I will climb higher
I will succeed
I will move forward

Cosmic Calligraphy   Born Free

I will move at a terrific speed
I will surprise myself and the world
I will join love's revolution
I will love even more
I will find a solution

The Devil Isn't Winning

The devil isn't winning
that's a false narrative
but prioritizing the word of God
is a global imperative
God's magnificence and power
is currently fighting against these wicked snakes
but which side are you on
which hand did you take

the devil isn't winning
but most believe he is
because most of the children of God
fear Satan's kids
I know that evil can't be completely stopped
but it can be put in check
God has already sent out the call
it's all hands and hearts on deck

the devil isn't winning
the tide can be turned
if we stopped letting God's world
slowly burn
the devil is living out his purpose
can God's people say the same
because if this world falls
it will be us and us alone that deserves all the blame

The Choice is Yours

The choice is yours
you want freedom or law
you signed the contract
but didn't see the hidden clause

now they got their claws
knuckles deep in your rectum
Farrakhan tried to warn us
way back at the Spectrum

but we ignored him
called it boredom
now new slave ships
sail down the digital river Jordan

now we needin the warden's endorsement
duckin pale horsemen
harassment, extortion
caught in a ghetto orbit

slow as a GMO tortoise
getting bullied like Norbit
it's morbid and sordid
lead inside the faucet

mentally amorphous
we need a deep catharsis
hug the heartless
help the harmless

Cosmic Calligraphy   Born Free

fight back regardless
this shit is straight garbage
we wail with the Wailers
and light up the darkness

I'm an arsonist
penmanship flawless
in love with a Goddess
we manifest God's promise

let's be honest
you need to pay homage
only the fearless
go through a metamorphosis

I'm merciless
flows cause turbulence
every word heard
reinforces my permanence

now back to my feature
that was just a teaser
a natural leader
I'm screaming death to Caesar

reload the street sweeper
I'm still a peacekeeper
an avid believer
baptized at Ebenezer

the poor righteous teacher
a true knowledge seeker
speakin Moses and Jesus
to my nephews and nieces

Cosmic Calligraphy　　　　　　　　　　Born Free

a sleeper cell
a church bell
a shooter in the stairwell
writing verses in brail

I know exactly why Rome fell
and how they broke the spell
they bombed the cartels
to dispel the false intel

and then propelled
up past the stars
beyond Mercury and Mars
God is inside each of these bars

all my books are memoirs
search inside the crevasses
for jewels and messages
fetishes and wild images

my thoughts are limitless
far from innocent
NEVER impotent
militant and INFINITE!

Untraditional

Untraditional
that's my favorite tradition
it keeps my eyes flexible
they never stiffen
they're never imprisoned
see all gifts and gryphons
I remember and listen
so my aura glistens
wisdom is in all things
not just my scriptures
God gave everyone a brush
to paint these pictures
we're all puzzle pieces
arrogance decreases
it's time to face the fact that
everything teaches

untraditional
that's my favorite tradition
it keeps me up to date
with the latest edition
whether I agree or disagree
that's not even the point
every way of life
has the power to anoint
if we just open up
and set another place at our table
we might discover that we have
a similar history, myth, legend, and fable
cuz we're all puzzle pieces
arrogance decreases
it's time to face the fact that
everything teaches

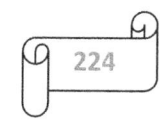

Get out of God's Way

Get out of God's way
he has something to say
Get out of God's way
he's trying to save you today
Get out of God's way
you're causing a delay
Get out of God's way
he's trying to save you today
Get out of God's way
Get out of God's way
Get out of God's way
Get out of God's way
Get out of God's way
Get out of God's way
Get out of God's way
Get out of God's way

I don't know everything
it doesn't matter what I read
the worse place I can be
is trapped inside my head
where I come to my own conclusions
reenforce illusions
an intelligent fool
with no evolution
a mister know-it-all
I was cocky, annoying
couldn't really build
cuz I was too busy destroying
toying with people
God warned me many times
I was doin too much
my mind was blind

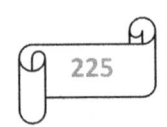

I had to remember what Grandma would say,

Get out of God's way
he has something to say
Get out of God's way
he's trying to save you today
Get out of God's way
you're causing a delay
Get out of God's way
he's trying to save you today
Get out of God's way
Get out of God's way
Get out of God's way
Get out of God's way
Get out of God's way
Get out of God's way
Get out of God's way
Get out of God's way

I'm a work in progress
don't let the dope flow fool you
I make mistakes daily
I'm just like you
I've worked hard and not smart
did less than my part
over invested in my brain
and shortchanged my heart
I still feel the pain of past deeds
still lost in the weeds
we all have angels and devils
which one do you feed
beloved, now I see
it's foolish to be at odds
victory came to me
when I let go and let God
so,

Get out of God's way
he has something to say
Get out of God's way
he's trying to save you today
Get out of God's way
you're causing a delay
Get out of God's way
he's trying to save you today
Get out of God's way
Get out of God's way
Get out of God's way
Get out of God's way
Get out of God's way
Get out of God's way
Get out of God's way
Get out of God's way

Not All

Not all Jedi's are all good
not all Sith are all bad
master this understanding
or you'll fall for the fad

truth is extremely nuanced
it lives and thrives on both sides
master this understanding
or your suffering will be multiplied

Don't Listen to Naysayers

Don't listen to naysayers
they come a penny a dozen
don't give them a vote or voice
in your discussions
they're typically jealous
a bitter rot grows within
and since they live among the condemned
they want to keep you down in hell with them

Journal Entry #26

The power of belief
won't change your life instantly
but without the power of belief
you can't change your life at all

L' Shana Tova

We're at the head of the year
starting over, no fear
it's time to put my life
in high gear

but first I give high praise
to the Creator of all creation
the Creator of all possibilities
the Creator of my transformation

as we head towards Yom Kippur
the walls changed into doors
the choice is before me again
and this time it won't be ignored

I must be better
I will be better
and it's not about memorizing
every word and letter

it's about my actions
it's about my consistent behavior
inaction is the only thing
that bring about failure

so, after I dip my apples in honey
and breathe divine sweetness in the air
L'Shana Tova
my actions will prove my words declared

Unclassified

Unclassified
is a part of the ways of Hashem
classified are the ways
of surface-dwelling women and men

definitions are necessary
within the mortal sphere
but the spiritually undefined
can experience the infinite crystal clear

I Wish You Heaven

I wish you Heaven
I pray that you follow your bliss
my reoccurring dream
is that you also want this

your beauty grows
with glorious strength and vigor
no matter your outside shape
the depth of your soul is incomparably bigger

I wish you Heaven
I pray that you reach within before you reach without
my reoccurring dream
is that the flowers within your heart begin to sprout

your beauty grows
with grace and fortitude
no matter what naysayers say
you have the Godly power to be renewed

Journal Entry #27

Once you actively personify
all of your Messiah concepts
your Messiah will instantly return
and be back in full effect

can you fathom this understanding
you are what you seek
when you visualize you materialize
your Messiah from your head to your feet

Wake Up, Get Up

Wake up, get up
wake up, get up
wake up, get up
wake up, get up
wake up, get up
wake up, get up
wake up, get up
wake up, get up
and DO!

You Won't Always Know the Way

You won't always know the way
things will get hectic and confusing
you might not always break
but you will experience some bruising

the truths that we seek
are not cinematic movie props
they don't magically make
all the pain and confusion stop

and I know faith in the face of darkness
challenges faith
Covid, Cancer, poverty, and homicide
makes us feel unsure and unsafe

but ironically
uncertainty can make the opposite case
chaos can become a crucible
that forges an even stronger faith

I don't have all the answers
I get lost
I feel fear
I feel turned around and tossed

I've felt the defeating pain of loss
I've cried so many bitter and clouded tears
but through it all
my faith is stronger than it's been in years

Journal Entry #28

Evil loves when we
pray in isolation
but when we collectively pray
through an outward practice
evil and his minions run back into the pits of hell

The Doer

I understand the Watchers
but I move with the Doers
fuck passive viewers
I'm a relentless pursuer
cuz if we're not getting involved
no problems get solved
and when nothing is evolved
the devil gets reinstalled
and just like the planets revolve
we must be in a constant state of movement
the Watchers provide the devil
with safety and amusement
the Watchers are voyeuristic
unrealistic
watching planetary death
makes them amoral and sadistic

the Watchers are the opposite of mystics
opposite of the godlike
watching and watching
helped install the Third Reich
watching and watching
is what helped our enslavement get 400 seasons
watching and watching
is why sickness has spread to every global region
I am a Doer
a demonstrator
the first seven seasons of Khaleesi
an emancipator
I am an excavator
a detonator
I'm how America sees the black man
a perpetrator

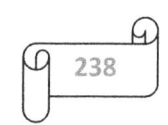

Cosmic Calligraphy   Born Free

I'm a Doer
I'm in the action frame of mind
my grind powers womankind
with Kyber crystal land mines
my time can't be calculated
Watchers are stagnated
overly debated
teenage boy masturbated
armchairs are outdated
completely overrated
if the ground isn't cultivated
all your seeds will be terminated
the Doers are the seeds of David
the Watchers are Esau's spawn
they talk like royal kings
but move like broken pawns

Listen

Listen carefully
God never stops speaking
everything in you and around you
is constantly teaching
keep yourself ready
keep yourself open
God's truth can be translated
in every tongue spoken and unspoken

Stay Loyal

Stay loyal to your dreams
even when it seems like all is lost
stay loyal to your vision
even when you don't have the money to cover the cost
stay loyal to your team
especially when all the money goes out or comes in
stay loyal to your God
especially when everything comes to an unexpected end
stay loyal
stay loyal
stay loyal
stay loyal

stay loyal to your heart
even when it falls in love with fools and villains
stay loyal to your mind
even when it turns you into a fool and villain
stay loyal to your goals
especially when your doubted at every turn and decision
stay loyal to your God
especially when your body is set free or imprisoned
stay loyal
stay loyal
stay loyal
stay loyal

Journal Entry #29

How in the fuck
did we get so far off course
black boys killing black boys
with absolutely no remorse
they post all their threats
live stream all their murders
snitchin is irrelevant
when your evil is on every IG server
the 80's and 90's
were the precursor
the 2000's marked the real murder
of our inner Malcom and Nat Turner
niggerism is the major threat to our lives
not cops or Covid
I'm afraid of what might have to happen
to save the majority of our kids

Close the Gaps

Close the gaps between us
we have no logical reason to be separated
tribe, gender, nation, or station
is no reason for a life to be stagnated

come closer to me
embrace me without fear
come closer to me
let the bullshit disappear

if we don't close the gaps
all this will collapse
all these lines on the map
are suicidal traps

don't let any more time elapse
we can make the future better or worse
close the gaps between us
God's love can slowly heal the hurt

The Book of Born Free

Denzel had The Book of Eli
Jabba's crew feared The Book of Boba Fett
but it's The Book of Born Free
that you really need to get

Mary emailed me The Kybalion
Luke lamented the sacred Jedi texts
but it's The Book of Born Free
that you really need to get

this isn't my ego talking
it's my loving heart
I wrote over 1,260 quotes
to stop us from falling apart

I respect all books
if they heal old and new wounds
but it's The Book of Born Free
that will prepare you for the hard times coming soon

From the Bottom of the Rabbit Hole

From the bottom of the rabbit hole
I can see the edges of the digital sky
machines making code into flesh
to make you believe your digital eyes

it's all a lie
you know the devil does that
he knows that Mario is weaker
when he loses his thinking cap

see the trap for what it is
don't follow the wrong footprints
check to see if it's any strings
attached to those gruesome gifts

green tint or no green tint
the Matrix is the Matrix by any other name
please make sure your new Messiah
isn't from inside the machine mainframe

Tend to your Garden

Tend to your garden
even if you haven't seen the sun in ages
tend to your garden
even if it contradicts your family and sages
tend to your garden
make it a prayer and not a labor
tend to your garden
and the rain will return the favor
tend to your garden
celebrate the dirt beneath your nails
tend to your garden
gardeners have the most balanced scales
tend to your garden
the peace you reap extends humanities lease
tend to your garden
plant your seeds between Gaia's heartbeats

God Told me to Release Them

My dreamcatchers caught a lot of visions
God told me to release them
you can't just read the hymns
the glory comes when you live them

God said, some might condemn your dreams
some might embrace
but no matter what they might do
never slow down your pace

when I read the scriptures
I hear them as instructions
over reading and over planning
are two of the biggest obstructions

what's the function of the lesson
what's the point of the jewels
being all show and no prove
is a self-enslaved game for fools

Journal Entry #30

Where is rock bottom
we've been free falling for decades
the payment to get paid
is a grotesque spiritual downgrade
we're in Satan's new crusade
the internet is the worst charade
black monster's wit choppers
in white supremacy's zombie brigade

Original People

We're original people
regal we kill eagles
born on the backs
of black scarab beetles

we were before the medieval
and we'll be here after the final upheaval
our lotus flowers
are both beautiful and lethal

I give birth to sequels
give shape to the mist
we will be here for ever
word to Kris

snakes don't always hiss
keep them away from adults and kids
more than Adam's life
they want to poison Adam's rib

we're original people
YAH's first creation
we are the foundation
of all nations

and since we're in this conversation
all that nigga shit is venomous
they want to take your excellence
cuz they fear your eminence

Cosmic Calligraphy   Born Free

we're at the precipice
of magnificence
focus your mind Lord
and get ready for the exodus

and snakes don't always hiss
keep them away from adults and kids
more than Adam's life
they want to clone Adam's rib

Are We Really

Are we really

going to let Branson, Bezos, and Musk
leave us on Earth
to rot and die in the dry dust
are we really
going to die squandering our resources
and putting our babies under the hoof's
of these pale horses
are we really
going to murder each other in this divided house
and buy more guns
just to blow are own brains out
are we really
going to betray our seeds time after time
just to impotently watch white billionaires
create and innovate and leave us behind

are we really
are we really
beloved, we look and sound
fuckin silly

are we really
are we really
beloved, we look and sound
fuckin silly

Journal Entry #31

Inhale the spirit of God
exhale the spirit of God
pray about the spirit of God
meditate deeply on the spirit of God
study the spirit of God
live the spirit of God
love the spirit of God
become one with the spirit of God

Penultimate

Penultimate verse
devils disperse
this is a lyrical infusion
come get immersed
I searched the universe
for new thoughts to construct
my life was pre-destined
I write to interrupt
the status-quo
the oppressor's peace of mind
I'm here to let you know
we're almost out of time
my books are more than just rhymes
more than just deep lines
I carry a message from Elohim
the supreme intelligent design

look around you
look inside
you know like I know
all these people didn't have to die
the murder rate is sky high
with no signs of abatement
it's a mistake to look at the word of God
as mere suggestions and past statements
what we think of as ancient
was a message to humanities future self
our ancestors saw this day coming
they tried to send us help
but we let the devil distract us
rewrite the narrative
add modified additives
now the adults bury their kids

Cosmic Calligraphy							Born Free

this system is rigged
disengage, disengage
the digital platform stage
is just another plantation and cage
but we can change
I know we can change
the cure for our sickness
must be obtained
new ground can be gained
but first we must retrain
our hearts, our souls
our minds, our brains
let's start a next level love campaign
self-sustained infrastructure domains
if a mustard seed of Gods flame remains
a better tomorrow can be attained and maintained

I KNOW WE CAN DO IT
I KNOW WE CAN DO IT
I KNOW WE CAN DO IT
I KNOW WE CAN DO IT
I KNOW WE CAN DO IT
I KNOW WE CAN DO IT
I KNOW WE CAN DO IT
I KNOW WE CAN DO IT

This Morning

If you woke up this morning
smile and say, THANK YOU!
if you woke up this morning
smile and say, I LOVE YOU!
and if you didn't wake up this morning
I am still concerned
cuz as I woke up this morning
I prayed for your soul's safe return

the first step
is opening your eyes
and realizing
that you made it back to this side
breathe in
breathe out
you made it back
without a doubt
be grateful
God gave you another gift
be grateful
God granted your wish
and no matter what happened yesterday
you can write something new on this fresh page
don't let anybody tell you
that you can't grow and change
so,

if you woke up this morning
smile and say, THANK YOU!
if you woke up this morning
smile and say, I LOVE YOU!
and if you didn't wake up this morning

Cosmic Calligraphy — Born Free

I am still concerned
cuz as I woke up this morning
I prayed for your soul's safe return

the next step
is making your first decision
will you choose peace or violence
you control the transmission
will you rise slowly
and say your prayers
or will you rush out the door
headfirst into the snares
what will you check on first
your spirit or your online feed
which will you nourish first
your wants or your needs
it's all up to you
how do you want to start this glorious day
don't let anybody fool you
you have a major say
so,

if you woke up this morning
smile and say, THANK YOU!
if you woke up this morning
smile and say, I LOVE YOU!
and if you didn't wake up this morning
I am still concerned
cuz as I woke up this morning
I prayed for your soul's safe return

THANK YOU FOR ALL THE LOVE, SUPPORT, AND INVESTMENT! I DON'T TAKE YOU FOR GRANTED!

Previous books by Born Free (Available on Amazon.com)

The Book of Born Free
The Wisdom of Living Right Now!
Volume One

Morning Wake Up Calls

Panther Poetry

The Book of Born Free
The Wisdom of Living Right Now!
Volume Two

A Citizen's Guide to Balancing *unbalanced*
POWER relationships
(Warnings & Instructions)

Schemers

Verses of Wine

Pyroclastic Flow

**Other books Published by
Conscious Commentary Publishing LLC**

Peace King! Can You Hear Me?
(Poems Inspired by The Love Thy Brotha Day Movement)

Nima Shiningstar-EL

Peace Queen! Can You Hear Me?
(Meditations Inspired by The Love Thy Brotha Day Movement)

Nima Shiningstar-EL

Nabbstract

Nima Shiningstar-EL

NIMA

Nima Shiningstar-EL

ABOUT THE AUTHOR

Carl Born Free Wharton was born and primarily raised in Philadelphia, Pennsylvania. He grew up in West Philly in a so-called "middle class" area called Wynnefield. He spent his formative years toggling in between the "Field" and down "The Bottom" at his Beloved Grandmother's (Pauline Ramsey) house on 38th & Poplar. The harsh dichotomies and undeniable similarities between these two neighborhoods taught and showed him graphically the range of black life during the 70's, 80's and 90's. He knew a life before the crack era and one after it struck. Witnessing the horror of this manufactured plague created inside his soul a relentless conscious perspective that was born to stand on the frontlines of the struggle for freedom, justice, and equality.

The fabric of his community was forever changed during the governmental assault of guns, drugs, and miseducation, and Born was determined to find out who was responsible for these horrendous crimes.

Since he was raised and came of age during Hip Hop's Cultural revolution, he understands the supreme importance of the written and spoken word.

His love of reading and exploring the great pantheon of black writers and other great literary figures set him on the path of becoming a lifelong scribe. Born wants to communicate and connect with the reader's heart by invoking raw emotions and holding up a mirror, so we can examine ourselves and the world around us.

In 2003 Born Free had ran into destiny when he met Malik One. He was a of member of KRS ONE's Temple of Hip Hop. Malik reached out about putting together a lecture at Temple University, under Michael Coard's Hip Hop 101 class. During that time Born meet and started working with KRS-ONE doing some street and online promotions. Soon after that, he became the Philadelphia Representative of KRS-ONE's Temple of Hip Hop. He booked lectures, interviews, and shows for different Hip Hop Legends at a variety of colleges and venues around the city. In 2004 Born had another date with destiny and met Wise Intelligent of the Legendary Poor Righteous Teachers and became a part of the foundation of Intelligent Muzik.

For the first 5 years of his time at Intelligent Muzik, Born wrote press releases, artists bio's, booked shows, negotiated contracts, created one sheets, and assisted on the creation of Intelligent Muzik's unique sound. While all that work was going on, Born was behind the scenes formulating an innovative writing project that would change the course of the current elementary literary style that has enveloped this very pregnant moment in time. Born Free has been blessed to work with a slew of Hip-Hop Legends and a gang of incredible artists in and out of Philly. He has worked directly with **KRS One, Public Enemy, Professor Griff, Wise Intelligent (PRT),**

Cosmic Calligraphy	Born Free

Cee Knowledge of Digable Planets, Narubi Selah (Def Poetry Jam), Nadria Norjahan, Killah Priest of the Wu-Tang Clan, J Rawls, Gensu Dean, Courtney Danger,

DJ SOYO, DJ Fusion, DJ Soulbuck, Magnum O, Natural Born Leaders, NYOIL, Hakim Green (of Channel Live) Nima ShiningStar-El, John Robinson, Eloh Kush, Dead Prez, and many many more giants of the culture and craft. Love is the connective tissue that unites everything that he does and writes about.

Love is the fire that burns brilliantly in his heart. Born loves to write and build on a variety of classical and contemporary ideas and thoughts but his greatest desire is to compel the reader to get the hell up and confront this life right here and right now! He started his own publishing company, **Conscious Commentary Publishing LLC.** in 2018 to ensure that he never has to water down his perspective or compromise his vision. The slogan of his company is crystal clear and straight to the point, **God Gave You a Voice, USE IT!** Born has released 8 projects to date. The first 5 written by Born are, **The Book of Born Free...The Wisdom of Living Right Now! Volume 1 & 2, Morning Wake Up Calls, Panther Poetry, and A Citizen's Guide to Balancing unbalanced POWER relationships (Warnings & Instructions)**. The 6th, 7th, and 8th books, **Peace King Can You Hear Me?, Peace Queen Can You Hear Me?** and **NIMA** published by **Conscious Commentary** and written by the talented **Nima ShiningStar-EL**,

At the end of the day, Born Free wants US to get up and activate our activism, and use our God given talents to bring love and light to a world increasingly becoming dark.

For more information about Born Free and all his new projects hit up https://www.instagram.com/therealbornfree
http://www.facebook.com/therealbornfree
http://www.twitter.com/therealbornfree

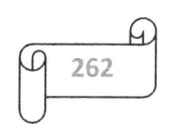

Conscious Commentary Publishing LLC
Contact Born Free @
therealbornfree@gmail.com

For interviews, articles, reviews, etc., contact Born Free @ therealbornfree@gmail.com

BUY Born Free's books from Amazon.com
linktr.ee/therealbornfree

REST IN PEACE
ROGER ERIC WHARTON

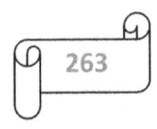

and please don't stop showing LOVE, LOVE!

Made in the USA
Coppell, TX
11 December 2021